"God is moving the human community into
to this need and opportunity? With fresh insi
reflection, Stephen Um and Justin Buzzard pı
the church can respond to this need. I'm tha
tion to this important subject!"

Mark Reynolds, Associate Director, Redeemer City to City

"The Bible is the story of a journey from a garden to a city. In the middle of it,
it's the story of the journey of the gospel from the city of Jerusalem to the city of
Rome, transforming them both. Stephen Um and Justin Buzzard helpfully trace
the journey, and prophetically show how it's possible to be part of the story."

John Ortberg, author; speaker; Senior Pastor, Menlo Park Presbyterian
Church, Menlo Park, California

"One can't effectively plant or pastor a church in an urban context without first
developing a theology of cities. This book will be an essential guide to discerning
leaders who know that cities matter and want to engage those cities well."

Ed Stetzer, President, LifeWay Research; author, *Subversive Kingdom*

"Recent years have witnessed a torrent of books on urbanization and on urban
ministry. Many of these are specialist sociological studies; others are 'how-to'
manuals so comprehensive that the Spirit of God could walk out and we'd never
miss him. What has been lacking is a short, reasonably comprehensive, impas-
sioned, and simply written survey of the trends and issues, combined with un-
wavering commitment to the eternal gospel and a transparent love for the city.
Whether or not you agree with all its details, this book supplies what has been
lacking. Written by two younger pastors on opposite sides of the country who
share their devotion to Christ and their years of fruitful ministry, this book is neither sociology nor manual (though it has some features of both), but a clarion call
to Christians to look at cities with fresh eyes and cry, 'Give me this mountain!'"

D. A. Carson, Research Professor of New Testament, Trinity Evangelical
Divinity School

"If you care about your city, the gospel, and the future of Christianity, I highly
recommend you read this insightful book by Justin Buzzard and Stephen Um. This
book should be required text for anyone doing ministry in today's world."

Stew Stewart, Founder and Director, Verge Network;
Pastor of Strategic Innovation, Austin Stone Community Church

"As cities go, so goes the world. We don't just need more Christians in cities, we
need better Christians who love where they live. This book shows the importance of cities and faithful city dwellers for the advancement of the gospel in the
twenty-first century."

Darrin Patrick, Lead Pastor, The Journey, St. Louis, Missouri;
author, *For the City and Church Planter: The Man, the Message, the Mission*

"It's only a matter of time. If you're a true follower of Jesus, very soon you will be a happy urbanite in a city called New Jerusalem. This book is a call to get a jumpstart on that civic future now, as we labor to secure an eternal city for others. We need Christians wherever there are people—rural, urban, and suburban—but urbanization is happening so quickly worldwide that the church is in need of a special summons to the cities. These two pastors from Boston and the Bay helped renew my sense of call to the Twin Cities, and likely will do the same for you in your locale—or be the catalyst for some new civic venture God is moving you toward in our increasingly urban world."

David Mathis, executive editor, desiringGod.org; elder, Bethlehem Baptist Church, Twin Cities, Minnesota

"Given the fact that more and more people are moving back to cities instead of away from them, a lot of books are being published on how the twenty-first-century church can reach the urban centers of the world. My friends Justin Buzzard and Stephen Um contribute to this necessary and strategic conversation by writing a book on *why* it's important to focus on cities. In the face of solid research that proves how culture-shaping cities are, Stephen and Justin call for missionary-mindedness—grounding that call, not in law-laden guilt, but in the radical done-ness of the gospel."

Tullian Tchividjian, Pastor, Coral Ridge Presbyterian Church in Ft. Lauderdale, Florida; author, *Jesus + Nothing = Everything*

"You don't need to live in a city to read this book. You don't even need to love the city to read this book. But you do need to know God loves the city, so the church should, too. Stephen Um and Justin Buzzard don't shy away from the problems of the city as they offer a hopeful and compelling agenda for the church in our urban future."

Collin Hansen, editorial director, The Gospel Coalition; coauthor, *A God-Sized Vision: Revival Stories That Stretch and Stir*

"Stephen Um and Justin Buzzard have done the church a great service in providing a clear and compelling argument not only for the importance of cities in our times, but more especially why cities matter to the church. They do a terrific job in teasing out a rich biblical theology of cities that roots their cultural analysis in a thoughtful and faithful framework. After reading the book, I wanted to call a real estate agent and tell them to find me a place in the city. It is not only where the 'cultural action' is today, but also where there is such a desperate need for thoughtful, faithful, and vibrant ministry. Um and Buzzard show us that cities are not to be shunned but loved with the full breath of the gospel. You will not be able to think about cities in the same old ways after reading this book."

Richard Lints, Vice President for Academic Affairs, Gordon-Conwell Theological Seminary

"*Why Cities Matter* drips with passion, not for cities primarily, but for the gospel and its spread in this world. Teeming with people, cities are strategic contexts for gospel living and gospel spreading. While urban church planting is a growing trend in many quarters of American evangelicalism today, the influx of people to major cities is growing even faster. Through this book, urban pastors will be steeled and reinvigorated in their calling, many future church planters will make a run for a city, and some suburban churches (like mine, I hope) will take their next church plant downtown. But this book is not just for current city-lovers and future urban church planters—neither is it just for pastors. Whatever your present or future context, this book will challenge you to think more strategically about your dwelling, vocation, and church for the cause of Christ in this world."

Ryan Kelly, Pastor for Preaching, Desert Springs Church, Albuquerque, New Mexico; Council Member, The Gospel Coalition

WHY
CITIES
MATTER

To God, the Culture, and the Church

**STEPHEN T. UM &
JUSTIN BUZZARD**

Foreword by Tim Keller

CROSSWAY

WHEATON, ILLINOIS

Why Cities Matter: To God, the Culture, and the Church

Copyright © 2013 by Stephen T. Um and Justin Buzzard

Published by Crossway
    1300 Crescent Street
    Wheaton, Illinois 60187

Cover design: Josh Dennis

First printing 2013

Printed in the United States of America

Trade paperback ISBN: 978-1-4335-3289-4
PDF ISBN: 978-1-4335-3290-0
Mobipocket ISBN: 978-1-4335-3291-7
ePub ISBN: 978-1-4335-3292-4

Library of Congress Cataloging-in-Publication Data

Um, Stephen T.
   Why cities matter to God, the culture, and the church /
foreword by Tim Keller ; Stephen T. Um and Justin Buzzard.
     p. cm.
   Includes bibliographical references and indexes.
   ISBN 978-1-4335-3289-4
   1. Cities and towns—Religious aspects—Christianity.
2. City missions. I. Buzzard, Justin, 1978–   II. Title.
BR115.C45U4   2013
270.09173'2—dc23   2012033799

Crossway is a publishing ministry of Good News Publishers.

VP		22	21	20	19	18	17	16	15	14	13
15	14	13	12	11	10	9	8	7	6	5	4	3	2	1

CONTENTS

FOREWORD

Tim Keller

Every week it seems I read more authors and scholars pointing to the increasing importance of cities, and arguing that the future of the world will be forged there. Jim Clifton, CEO and Chairman of Gallup, points to the shrunken GDP (gross domestic product) of the United States and the vast shortfall in new job creation. What is the solution? He writes,

> If you were to ask me, "From all the data you have studied so far, where will the next breakthrough, such as Internet-based everything, come from?" my answer would be: from the combination of the forces within big cities, great universities, and [their] powerful local leaders. . . . The cornerstone of these three is cities . . . [as] goes the leadership of the top 100 American cities, so goes the country's economic future.[1]

Recently *The Guardian* newspaper in Great Britain did a special issue, "The Future of Cities." One writer opined, "Just 10 years ago, cities were seen as vital contributors to the global economy. That's no longer true. Today, cities *are* the global economy . . . the 40 largest cities, or mega-regions, account for two-thirds of the world's output."[2] The issue presented the following statistics:

- According to the United Nations, almost 180,000 people move into cities across the world every day. That is nearly 5.5 million people a month, or a new San Francisco Bay Area being created every 30 days.
- Fifty percent of Africa's population will be urban by 2050. The figure currently is 38 percent.
- In the next 20 years, China's cities will add an additional 350 million people to their current population, more than the entire population of the United States.

- Twenty-two percent of the world's population lives in 600 cities, and these 600 cities generate 60 percent of the world's GDP.
- There are currently 23 megacities with over 10 million in population; by 2025 there will be 36.[3]

The journal *Foreign Policy* did a special issue on cities near the end of 2010, announcing, "The age of nations is over. The new urban age has begun." The lead article announced, "The 21st century will not be dominated by America or China, Brazil or India, but by the city. In an age that appears increasingly unmanageable, cities rather than states are becoming the islands of governance on which the future world order will be built. . . . Neither 19th-century balance-of-power politics nor 20th-century power blocs are useful in understanding this new world. Instead, we have to look back nearly a thousand years, to the medieval age in which cities such as Cairo and Hangzhou were the centers of global gravity, expanding their influence confidently outward in a borderless world."[4]

Albert Mohler, president of The Southern Baptist Theological Seminary in Louisville, KY, read through the 2010 special report—"The Future of Cities"—by the *Financial Times,* and he responded with some strong language.

> This much is clear—the cities are where the people are. In the course of less than 300 years, our world will have shifted from one in which only 3 percent of people live in cities, to one in which 80 percent are resident in urban areas. If the Christian church does not learn new modes of urban ministry, we will find ourselves on the outside looking in. The Gospel of Jesus Christ must call a new generation of committed Christians into these teeming cities. As these new numbers make clear, there really is no choice.[5]

As most readers can see, all of these claims about the crucial importance of the city come from wildly divergent voices. Jim Clifton's book is intensely pro–United States and pro-business. His dominating concern is that America maintains its fast-eroding economic leadership in the world. *The Guardian, Financial Times,* and *Foreign Policy* are secular British and international publications—not at all conservative in their outlook—and are interested in not only economics, but the future of politics and culture. Al Mohler is a seminary president. His concern is the mission of the church. He wants to take the gospel to the world in such a way that it can have the greatest impact and see the most people converted.

Completely different people and different concerns. And yet, remarkably, they all agree on the crucial importance of cities. They all argue that "as cities go, so goes the world," and that to go to cities is necessary for anyone who wants to have an impact on how life is lived in this world.

This is especially true for those, like Al Mohler, who want to win as many as possible to Christ. Christians, particularly in America, are generally negative toward cities. Several mission executives have told me over the years that we need to send missionaries to the fast growing cities of the world (as well as to the regenerating cores of Western cities), but very few American Christians have lived in urban centers or even like them. We need churches everywhere there are people, but the people of the world are moving into the great cities of the world *much* faster than the church is. And therefore we must call Christians to better understand and care for cities, and we must call more Christians to consider living and ministering in cities.

This book by my friends Stephen Um and Justin Buzzard addresses all of these concerns. It not only makes a case for "why cities matter" but also helps readers understand the distinct ways in which cities operate, and how ministry and life can thrive there. I'm delighted that both of these men are bringing their wisdom and experience to bear on this issue. They have produced a volume that is accessible yet biblically and theologically well grounded. Learn from it. Enjoy it!

ACKNOWLEDGMENTS

Stephen Um:

Much appreciation is due to the session of Citylife Presbyterian Church (Boston, MA). Their love for our church and city, as well as their personal support, propelled this book into publication.

Tim Keller's fingerprints are all over this book. As a dear friend and mentor for many years, he has influenced my understanding of the city more than anyone. Thankfully, he not only shaped my thinking, but also helped me to grow in my love for cities. Thanks, Tim.

Similarly, my colleagues at Redeemer City to City have taught me much about cities. I am indebted to Terry Gyger, Jay Kyle, Mark Reynolds, Al Barth, John Thomas, and Gary Watanabe for the ways in which they have increased my love for cities throughout the world.

The ongoing partnership in the gospel that I share with Mark Younger and his family is a consistent source of encouragement. His burden for the gospel and cities is exemplary. Thank you, Mark.

I would like to thank my personal assistant, Justin Ruddy, who has owned this project from the very beginning. His theological insights were extremely important in formulating the overall argument for the book. I could not ask for a better ministry partner than Justin.

Finally, and most importantly, my wife Kathleen, along with my three daughters, is just as much responsible for the origination of this book as I am. Having lived in New York City for many years, she developed a love for cities way before I did. Her wisdom is woven into the fabric of this book. Your endurance, love, and support allowed me the time and space to write *Why Cities Matter*. Your perseverance and care have resulted in what I hope will be a small contribution in helping people gain a greater appreciation and love for cities.

Justin Buzzard:

I want to thank my city and my church for helping me write this book. As I live life in Silicon Valley alongside the people of Garden City Church, I'm learning so much about following Jesus and impacting our city for Jesus. Silicon Valley is an exciting and dynamic place to live; it challenges me every week. And Garden City Church is a thrilling church to lead—our wonderful people, difficult mission, and the weight of leadership both bless me and stretch me every week. I'm excited about the lifetime of learning I have ahead of me. Most days I feel like an ambitious and eager kindergartner headed to his first day of school. I have so much to learn about life in our city, and I can't wait to learn it.

At night I often dream about the great work God could do in our city and in the great cities of our world. I pray this book stirs you to dream big and pray big about what God might do in your city.

INTRODUCTION

The city is more important than ever. Right now, more people live in cities than at any other time in human history. Never before has the majority of the world's population been an urban population.

Cities have always played a central role in human history. Cities have long stood as powerful places of cultural development, influence, and invention—offering hope, refuge, and new beginnings. But never before have cities been as populated, powerful, and important as they are today.

The world is changing. Our world is experiencing the largest movement of urban growth in history. Our world is now predominantely urban, and there's no going back. This new reality, this new world, presents a historic opportunity for Christians.

Cities shape the world. What happens in cities doesn't stay in cities. What happens in cities spreads—as the city goes, so goes the broader culture. Think of cities like you think of a factory. What is produced in the factory (city) gets shipped outside the factory and distributed throughout the world. The products shipped by the factory shape life far beyond the walls of the factory. Cities ship and shape. Cities are important because they possess a far greater "shipping" and "shaping" power than any other human settlement, such as a suburban community or a country village.

Cities are the center of cultural and economic development in our twenty-first-century world. Cities produce the people, economic resources, businesses, art, universities, political policies, and research and development—the cultural goods—that shape and define our modern society. What happens in London or Hong Kong today will affect the American financial market more than what happens in the suburbs of Chicago. Tomorrow's technological innovation in Silicon

Valley will soon impact Manila, Tokyo, and Cape Town, along with their respective countries and neighboring communities.

Cities no longer shape just their surrounding regions—they now shape the whole world. This new world presents Christians and the church with an unprecedented opportunity to bring the gospel of Jesus Christ into every dimension of human life.[1] God is doing something new and big in our cities, and he's calling some of us to participate in it.

It is our opinion that books about the city have often misunderstood and misrepresented the city. Much Christian literature about the city has focused merely on inner-city problems (crime, the homeless, etc.) and how an urban ministry might fix these problems, rather than providing a comprehensive analysis of the city. Intentionally or unintentionally, cities have been portrayed as places of problem, rather than places of opportunity and blessedness. The reality is bigger and more beautiful than what the evangelical portrayal has typically shown— the city is a wonderful, dynamic, exciting, and healthy place for people to live, work, and make a difference. The default definition with which many Christians seem to have grown up—"cities are uncomfortable, congested places filled with crime, grime, and temptation"—is a definition we hope to dislodge and disinfect throughout this book.[2]

Cities are diverse, dense places where different types of people interact with one another. Cities are populated with people of various cultures, different worldviews, and different vocations. Cities force individuals to refine their cultural assumptions, religious beliefs, and sense of calling as they rub up against the sharp edges of the assumptions, beliefs, and expertise of other city dwellers. A twenty-something from a small, white, upper-middle-class, churchgoing Midwestern suburb who has a desire to teach high school students meets a tremendous opportunity for growth when he moves into center-city Boston. He will become a new type of teacher when he holds his first day of class and finds students of every conceivable race, culture, social standing, and worldview. Encounters take place in cities that do not take place elsewhere.

Cities are not places of sameness. Nothing ever stays the same in cities. There is constant movement. With the majority of the world's population now living in cities, cities are places where the world's population gathers to do life, business, and education. This rich, diverse DNA of the city creates an environment where tremendous culture making can take place. Though this environment can also lead to idol making and cultural pride, the city has always been central to God's plans for his people. The city stands as one of our great hopes for renewing our broken world.

Because the Bible's first reference to a city is a city built by Cain the fugitive (Gen. 4:17), we tend to think that cities are an unfortunate product of the fall. This assumption is the result of a misreading of the Bible's story line. The Bible teaches that the city is God's idea, invention, and intention.

Our triune God created man and woman in his image to be representatives of his presence on earth. After creating the first man and woman, God commissioned them with a vocation to fulfill. In essence, God called upon humanity to continue doing what God himself had been doing—to create. God gave man and woman the Cultural Mandate—a calling to be fruitful, to multiply, to fill the earth, and to cultivate and develop the garden. This mandate was ultimately an urban mandate, a call to create settlements where people could live and work together to be fruitful, to multiply, to develop, to cultivate, and to flourish.

The city is a natural and intended outgrowth of the flourishing community that our triune God has always enjoyed with himself as Father, Son, and Spirit, and of the culture-making mandate he gave to the first human settlers. When God's Son came to the earth, he took up residence in an earthly city. And when Jesus returns to the earth, he will bring with him a new city, a "holy city" where God and man will dwell together (Revelation 21). The Bible invites some of us to be city people, to engage our cities just as Jesus did, to make meaningful contribution to the commerce and culture of our cities.

People tend to adopt one of two approaches to the city. Some people retreat from the city. Thinking cities are dangerous and intimidating places, they venture into the city only when it's absolutely necessary for them to do so. Other people use the city. Thinking cities are exciting and beneficial places, they use the city to gain all they can—be it wealth, credentials, work experience, a change of scenery, or a tourist's sampling of various cultural goods.

The Scriptures invite us to relate to the city in an uncommon way. The Bible invites us to engage, to settle down in, and to contribute to our cities (Jeremiah 29). Instead of retreating from our cities, we're encouraged to understand and engage with what is happening in the city. Instead of touring our cities, we're invited to put roots down into our cities. Instead of merely taking from our cities, we're invited to contribute to the life and development of our city—be it through art, business, law, literature, music, medicine, education, finance, etc. The Bible's invitation is for us to seek the common good of our city. It's a countercultural call. It's a call to see the city as our home, and to take good care of it.

The cities of our world are growing in size and influence, and they stand in need of thoughtful Christians and churches to take up residence in them. If our culture is to be renewed with the gospel, if our world is to be restored, then we must reach our cities.

We live in a unique moment in history. At no other time in history has our world looked so similar to the setting of the early church. Read the book of Acts and you read about a world that looks much like our own—an urban, pluralistic, cosmopolitan, diverse, dynamic, rapidly changing, and fast-developing world. Two thousand years ago, God built his church through cities. The book of Acts is a story about the geographic expansion of the gospel through cities. Jerusalem, Ephesus, Corinth, and Rome represent where the gospel was preached, disciples were made, and churches were established. These cities became healthier communities because Christians were there.

These cities were engaged strategically so that surrounding regions could be reached. Today's world is similar, only today if you reach a city then you reach the world. Never before has the majority of the world's population been a city population. Never before have urban centers held such significance and power. What we're witnessing is both similar to and grander than the world inhabited by the early church. The opportunity is staggering. What God did two thousand years ago is something that God can do again today. In fact, God can do something even greater in our day—for he is God, and our cities offer tremendous potential for gospel growth.

We don't say this lightly or approach this moment casually. We've written this book as practitioners. We are putting to the test everything we've written here. We're both church planters leading churches in influential cities, and we've banked our livelihood on God and his power to do a redeeming work in our respective cities.

Aside from our shared love for the gospel, cities, and the church, and the fact that we're both tall, we don't have much else in common. Everything else about us is different, and we believe this is a strength in coauthoring a book like this—we both write as practitioners, but as practitioners with different life experiences.

Stephen is from the East Coast; Justin is from the West Coast. Stephen lives in Boston—the academic hub of the world; Justin lives in Silicon Valley—the innovation hub of the world. Stephen is an Asian-American who understands the intrinsic challenges of being part of a minority culture; Justin is a white-American who grew up as a member of the majority culture. Stephen is in his mid-forties; Justin is in his early thirties. Stephen has led a thriving Presbyterian church in center-city Boston for ten years; Justin, after ten years of pastoral ministry, just planted a nondenominational church in the heart of Silicon Valley that's only a year old. Stephen wears suits; Justin wears T-shirts. Stephen has three daughters; Justin has three sons. On and on we could go.

In short, we are good friends who are excited about what God is doing in our world's cities. We wrote this book with the hope that others would see and share in this strategic work that is increasingly city-centered, so that more and more believers might have a deep vision for a global movement of the gospel in cities.

Here's where we're headed in the coming pages. The first chapter seeks to answer the question, "*What* is the importance of cities in our world today?" We consider the past, present, and future of cities, along with some basic categories for identifying a city. Chapter 2 looks at the way that cities function, and asks, "*Why* do cities play such a crucial role in our world?" We find that there are several common characteristics that explain the cultural prominence of cities in our world today. The crucial task of determining what the Bible says about cities is taken up in chapter 3. Then, in the last three chapters, we consider various issues that face those seeking to minister in our world's cities: chapter 4 looks at the topic of contextualization; chapter 5 explores how we should relate to our city's dominant story line; and chapter 6 thinks through the development of a ministry vision for your city.

Chapter 1

THE IMPORTANCE OF CITIES

> What will be remembered about the twenty-first century
> . . . is the great, and final, shift of human populations out of
> rural, agricultural life and into cities. We will end this cen-
> tury as a wholly urban species.[1]
>
> Doug Saunders

A VIEW FROM THE CITY

It's ten o'clock on a Sunday morning. A PhD student at one of the top research universities in the world swipes her subway card and hops on a Red Line subway train headed for center-city Boston. As she does, she leaves the fifth-highest-ranked school in America, home to seventy-seven past and present Nobel Prize Laureates.[2] Had she gone two stops in the opposite direction she would have found herself at Harvard. But she's headed for center city to worship with her church. Crossing the Charles River, she gets off at the next stop to connect with a friend who is just finishing a twenty-four-hour shift. He's an endocrinology resident at Massachusetts General Hospital, one of the oldest, most respected hospitals in America.[3] A professing skeptic, he's a bit uncomfortable with organized religion, but the apparent normality of two Christian coworkers has made him more open to conversations about faith. Together, they ride one more stop to Park Street Station, walk through the oldest public park in America (Boston Common),[4] skim the edge of the historic Theater District, and take an elevator to the sixth floor of a hotel, where they're just in time for corporate worship at a church planted only ten years ago.

Surgeons, lawyers, psychiatrists, athletes, musicians, teachers, investors, venture capitalists, professors, bakers, engineers, nurses, entrepreneurs, techies, and students en route to an even wider variety of vocations—all are gathered from around the city to hear and interact with the gospel. They come from a wide variety of ethnic, religious, and socioeconomic backgrounds. Many are new Christians. Nearly one out of every five is a confessing skeptic investigating the claims of the Christian faith. At the close of the service they will disperse throughout the city. Some will walk a few blocks for a meal in Chinatown; others will rush to Fenway Park to see the first pitch of an early afternoon Red Sox game. The city pulses with the energy of theater and live music, bustling shopping districts and booming financial centers, along with innovation and creativity that continually lead to breakthroughs in medicine, technology, and the arts.

Additional landmarks, hospitals, universities, and companies could be referenced, but perhaps more remarkable than these highlights themselves is the fact that they are all packed snuggly into a two-mile radius that approximately 225,000 people call home.[5] Even more, this radius is simply a part of a larger city. It acts as the hub of the greater Boston area—home to 4.6 million people.[6] What is it that gives this small patch of land such prominence? What led to such concentration of power and influence? Why the centralization of innovation and creativity? To answer these questions is to get at what it is that makes cities so vitally important on a variety of levels.

And so, in this chapter we hope to explore these and other questions about just *what* it is that makes cities important. What is their place in our world today? What role have cities played in our history? Will cities significantly shape our future? What opportunities and challenges do gospel churches face in cities? Difficult questions, yes, but necessary and exciting, nonetheless.

Remarkably, what we have described in Boston is not a unique phenomenon. We see people crowding together in cities more often than not. This happens throughout the world, and often on a much larger scale. It would seem that humans have a propensity for crowding together in densely populated, energy filled cities, even when wide-open, livable places are available and accessible. And, when we crowd together, big things happen. "On a planet with vast amounts of space, we choose cities."[7]

As we proceed in this chapter we'll consider the history of cities, projections about our cities, and just what it is that makes a city a city.

THE PAST LIFE OF CITIES

In some sense, humans have always crowded together in cities. From the early chapters of Genesis, people are seen to be city builders. Within a generation of leaving the garden of Eden, humankind was building cities. This shows that city building has always been a part of our nature (Gen. 4:17). And when we look to broader world history, we find that cities have long been with us; they have always held an important place in human culture.

Though the particulars of the origins of the city are somewhat hazy (just as the details of early human history are hazy), we do know that religion was essential to all early settlements. Primitive urban societies are best characterized as shrine city-states.[8] No matter the society or religion, priestly classes were instrumental in the establishment of the first urban settlements, and religious structures were consistently found at the center of the earliest cities. Wrapped up with a culture's religion were its commerce, politics, and power. In other words, the things that make a city a city—a place that is "sacred, safe, and busy"[9]—were initially developed and managed by religious leaders and institutions. This central role of religion has led urbanists to view it as the prime, organizing principle for the first cities—"the city's ultimate reason for existence."[10] The earliest examples of such shrine city-states date to around 5000 BC. Though much smaller than the modern megacities to which we have referred, all of the essential ingredients of an urban society were in place.[11]

Following this embryonic stage, cities developed on a much larger scale and at a faster pace. The first major wave of urbanization began with the rise of imperial cities that functioned as capital cities for larger states and empires.[12] Babylon would be the first of these cities to ascend to legendary status. Readers of the Bible will know it as the primary foe of the city and people of God (Jeremiah 20–21; Revelation 18). Also crucial was Alexander the Great's imperial vision that led to the development of Seleucia, Antioch, and "the first . . . universal city, the supreme Hellenistic melting pot"—Alexandria.[13] However, the greatest achievement of this initial wave of urbanization was the first megacity: Rome.

As readers of biblical and church history know, the capital city of the Roman Empire played a crucial role in world history. It would continue to be the dominant city on the urban horizon until near the end of the fifth century AD, when the fall of Rome would leave Constantinople as the only remaining imperial city. Following Rome's fall, cities developed throughout the Eastern world in places like China and Egypt, but the Western world experienced the Dark Ages.[14] It is no coincidence that the darkest period of Western history coincides with the relative absence of cities. Without the safety, economy, and sacred space of developing urban centers, individuals were left to fend for themselves—decline was to be expected.

The second major wave of urbanization occurred in the middle to late Medieval era, when population, commerce, culture, and education were on the rise in European cities like Paris, Venice, and Milan.[15] In these growing cities, religion continued to be a centralizing structure; "at the heart of the medieval city was the cathedral."[16] Yet, this was also a period of transition, when commerce began to emerge as a new organizing structure for cities.[17] New social and economic freedoms led to the growth of cities, and then naturally to the questioning of the reigning religious power structure: the Catholic Church. It was at the height of this wave of urbanization that the Protestant Reformation occurred. It was "a uniquely urban event."[18] With the invention of the printing press, tracts and Bibles spread throughout densely populated cities and towns. The reaffirmation of the priesthood of all believers, along with the validation of secular vocation, created a new ethic for urban life—one that would help pave the way for urban advancements in technology, production, and social life for future centuries.[19]

What came next in the historical life of cities? On the heels of expanding religious freedoms, growing commercial markets, and the questionable colonization of vast parts of India, Africa, and South America came the third wave of urbanization: the industrial city. Propelled by the Industrial Revolution's innovations in machinery, transportation, and production methods, on the whole, the population and wealth of cities exploded. By default, commerce became the new center of the city. Modern-day urban giants like London and New York had their major boons in this period.[20] By the early twentieth century, the phenomenon of the industrial city had spread around the globe, leading to the incredible growth of cities like Tokyo, Berlin, and St. Petersburg.[21] However, along with this urban progress came urban decay. Because cities function as a magnifying glass for humanity, displaying our best and worst potential, one might argue that the grand scale of the atrocities of the twentieth century was partly dependent on the grand scale of the cities in which they took place. Furthermore, the industrial city was simply not sustainable. A look at industrial cities like Detroit and Buffalo, which to this point have had difficulty reinventing themselves, shows us that a city will not thrive if it places a higher premium on material production than human innovation.

Cities have been with us since the beginning. But will they remain? Will all cities ultimately follow the path of slow decline that we see in many industrial cities? Or does recent history give us reason to hope that cities on the whole are on an upward trajectory? Where do we presently stand, and where are we headed?

THE PRESENT LIFE OF CITIES AND OUR URBAN FUTURE

As you read this book, we find ourselves in the middle of the fourth and greatest wave of urbanization; it is being identified as the era of the megacity, the megalopolis, the postcolonial city, and the global city.

Today's reality is that cities are larger, more diverse, more powerful, more innovative, and more global than ever, and they are advancing faster than they have ever done in the past. From Shanghai to Moscow, London to Mumbai, New York to Seoul, São Paulo to Cairo, the world has never been more urban. Humanity's march toward the city has reached a new benchmark. In 1900 only 14 percent of the world's population lived in urban areas; that number had grown to 30 percent by 1950. In 2008 the world's population was evenly split between urban and rural areas, but in 2011 the world became predominantely urban.[22] The numbers are even more striking in developed areas where, on average, 74 percent of the population lives in urban areas.[23]

The facts about our present situation are undeniable, but questions naturally arise: Is the massive scale of urbanization accidental, or has a pattern emerged that will continue to shape our world in the coming years? Have cities reached their peak, leaving the pendulum to swing back toward a rural, agrarian society? Or will the momentum of urbanization move us into a future that is increasingly urban?

While prognostications have no sway over the future, "the most reliable predictions are those that follow established trends."[24] In this regard, the undeniable trends of the twentieth and early twenty-first centuries have led researchers, with few known exceptions, to conclude that in the twenty-first century and beyond, our world will become increasingly urban. For example, the UN Population Division's massive study on World Population Prospects suggests that by 2050 the world will be 68.7 percent urban.[25] In more developed regions, the number is likely to reach 86.2 percent.[26] Amazingly, "by mid-century, the world urban population will likely be the same size as the world's total population was in 2004."[27] These predictions are astounding in describing the urban shape of our future.

The growth is charted to occur on the largest scale in the developing world. In Asia for instance, between 2009 and 2050, cities will move from representing 41 percent of the population to 64 percent. Essentially, rural populations will decrease by approximately 531 million, while urban populations will increase by 1.67 billion.[28] Further evidence of this coming shift can be found in China's recent transition to becoming a majority urban nation.[29] In many respects this is something to celebrate, particularly in light of the fact that "there is a near-perfect correlation between urbanization and prosperity across nations."[30] Of course, new challenges and problems will emerge, but cities have a unique way of creating solutions to their problems. Our world's economic wealth, technological innovation, and cultural development are based in part on the city's ability to examine its own urban condition. And there is no reason to believe that cities will fail to generate answers to their questions.

In short, all signs point to a *very* urban future. What do we need to know about cities in order to live well in this future? What should we make of the increasing concentration of power in urban centers? What makes cities so influential in our culture? What kind of opportunities does major urbanization present for the spread of the gospel? The rest of the chapter will seek to answer some of these questions, while giving big categories on which to hang our thoughts about the structure, meaning, and purpose of cities.

THE MAKINGS OF A CITY

The past, present, and potential future show us that cities are dynamic communities, which come in numerous shapes and sizes. What they all share in common is a large number of people freely choosing to dwell closely with one another. This is the essence of cities: cities emerge when people choose to live, work, and play in close proximity to one another. Edward Glaeser's definition is helpful here: "Cities are the absence of physical space between people. . . . They are proximity, density, closeness."[31] He would even go so far as to claim that "cities are people."[32] We think he's right.

If cities are people choosing to live in close proximity to one another, what reasons can be given for why human beings choose to do this more often than not? Joel Kotkin, author of *The City: A Global*

History, suggests three overarching categories for understanding what leads people to create cities: they keep us *safe*, they keep us *social*, and they shape our understanding and awareness of the *sacred*.[33] To put it another way, cities are centers of power, culture, and spirituality. In what follows, we will develop these three categories as we seek to answer the question, *what makes a city a city?*

Cities Are Centers of Power

History shows that one of the driving forces behind the advent of the city was the need for safety. Speaking about the earliest examples of cities, Harvie Conn links this notion of refuge with the idea of the city as the seat of power:[34] "Its walls marked it as protector . . . whether small or large the city-state was the anvil of civilization, the center of power."[35] In short, the search for safety in a lawless world led people to band together to create structures that would keep them safe. Walls, militaries, laws, government, and commerce are important elements of a safe human society, and they were all developed by cities. Today, these structures and their descendants are the means by which power is measured.

It is true that most members of developed societies have ceased to think of cities as places of refuge and safety, but the constant movement of immigration to developed cities by persons from less developed regions suggests that cities continue to play this role in our world. The opportunity to live in a well-governed society, to earn a reasonable wage, and to dwell in a well-built residence, continues to lead millions of individuals to leave their rural homes for the world's cities. In many ways, urbanization is the result of migration to centers of power.[36]

When the structures are set in place for the proliferation of safety, wealth, and good governance, cities thrive. Using the United States as an example, it is no surprise that the center of its government and defense spawned a city (Washington, DC). Nor should it shock us that all of its other major cities grew up around the potential for economic gain (New York, Boston, Chicago, Los Angeles, etc.). People flock to cities for safety and refuge. They remain in cities to gain proximity to these power structures, and once people settle into cities then they think of ways to make meaningful contribution to their advancement.

A look at the economic importance of cities is just one way of measuring the concentration of power in urban places. According to Richard Florida, "In the United States, more than 90 percent of all economic output is produced in metropolitan regions, while just the largest five metro regions account for 23 percent of it."[37] On a global scale, the world economy is driven largely by forty metropolitan megaregions. The top ten megaregions, home to just 6.5 percent of the world's population, produce 43 percent of the world's economic output.[38] Remarkably, the economic output of a highly developed megacity like New York eclipses the entire economic output of developing countries like Mexico and India.[39] It is true that in discussing the concentration of economic output we cannot avoid the issues of inequality and poverty. However, as we will see in chapter 2, cities do not make people poor, but rather they attract poor people because they offer greater opportunities for escaping poverty.[40] "For most people, cities are the solution, not the problem."[41]

In pointing out these astonishing numbers, we simply hope to illustrate the level of concentrated influence and power that is present in cities. We are not saying that Christian mission should be defined by the power structures of our day. In fact, if the gospel is present in our cities, it will not shy away from challenging the prevailing abuses and misuses of power. Nor are we saying that places with higher economic output have more intrinsic value than others, or are more qualified recipients of the gospel. Rather, we hope that we've been able simply to illustrate the importance of cities in our world today. As centers of power that provide safety, government, and economic opportunity, cities will continue to be magnets for an increasing majority of the world's population. The question is, will gospel churches and Christians be present when the world arrives in the city?

If the concentration of power is one mark of a city, another is the centralization of cultural capital.

Cities Are Centers of Culture[42]

When we ask the question, "What is it that makes cities important?" a major theme that quickly emerges is that cities are centers of culture. To understand this, all one needs to do is consider the shape of everyday life. For example, in the Western world, popular music tends to be created, produced, and performed in cities before extending its reach into everyday life in the suburbs. Even the majority of country music, which often romantically glorifies small-town life by poking fun at city living, is produced in a city (Nashville). The same can be said about television and film (Los Angeles, Mumbai), fashion (New York, Paris, Milan), technology (Silicon Valley, Tokyo), and education (Boston). Want to see the best in live theater? You'll have to go to the nearest urban center. Your favorite sports team? It's located in a city. The best symphony, museums, research, world-class restaurants? They are almost always in cities. Your cell phone, e-reader, computer, household appliances, and car? Again, likely designed or produced in cities.[43]

Why stack up all of these examples? Is this just city propaganda? No. We don't think so. Whether you find yourself cheering for cities, or feeling suspicious of them, the reality is that they are the primary shapers of the culture in which we live. If you have adopted any of the conveniences of our modern culture, you are not only the beneficiary but also a dependent recipient of the culture that is produced in cities. And so to eliminate the city is to eliminate culture—*your* culture. Conversely, to enter the city is to enter the culture's creative engine.

What we're suggesting here is a move beyond the typical dichotomous approach ("city v. suburbs") of understanding the importance of cities. That distinction has been unhelpful for as long as it has dominated discussions about cities and the regions that develop around them. What we might consider, instead, is a more robust understanding of the interplay that exists between cities and nonurban communities. Take, for instance, Kotkin's recent article, "Why America's Young and Restless Will Abandon Cities for Suburbs."[44] There he suggests that a significant number of the twenty-five- to thirty-four-year-olds that make up a typical urban population will move out to the suburbs by the time they become thirty-five- to forty-four-year-olds. The proposed reason for this move is that "when 20-somethings get older, they do things like marry, start businesses, settle down and maybe start having kids." Fair enough. But the question is, how do we process and respond to this information?

If we approach this thesis from one side of the "city v. suburbs" debate, we may find ourselves saying, "Aha! The city is not on the rise after all. The majority of people will end up in the suburbs in the end." The other side might bemoan the flight of the privileged, or simply look down on those who have cast their vote for sprawl. However, a more reasonable view is that there is a dialogue or interplay that exists between city and suburb, and that this piece of the dialogue actually goes further in making the case for "city as the center of culture" than any other.

Not only do the suburbs receive culture shaped by the city, they receive *people* shaped by the city. And, though they have relocated to the suburbs, these individuals likely work in the city, are fed a cultural diet delivered to their doorstep by the city, succeed in the suburbs based on skills acquired in cities, and shape their lives and the world around them with the ideologies acquired during their formative years in the city. We can be certain that, in the midst of a global population boom with cities at its center, the world's suburbs will become increasingly influenced by the cities to which they are connected. More than ever before, it is now the case that "as the city goes, so goes the culture."[45]

Cities as Centers of Worship

The discussion of the city's influence becomes further intensified when we consider that cities also function as centers of worship. It was the great urban historian Lewis Mumford who claimed that this religious element of the city preceded even the economic and physical elements. "The first germ of the city . . . is in the ceremonial meeting place . . . because it concentrates . . . certain 'spiritual' or supernatural powers, powers . . . of wider cosmic significance than the ordinary processes of life."[46] The sacred aspect of the city stands "as the very reason for the city's existence, inseparable from the economic substance that makes it possible."[47] Cities are built upon the things from which humanity attempts to derive its ultimate significance. Whether centered around a mosque or a financial district, a cathedral or an entertainment sector, all cities are built in honor of and pay homage to some type of a "god."

Many have bemoaned the advent of the skyscraper and its overshadowing visage over the traditional church steeple as signaling the demise of religion.[48] Yet, while it is true that Western culture has increasingly distanced itself from organized religion, there is a sense in which we remain just as spiritual as ever. As authors like Tim Keller and David Powlison have reminded us, the default, irreversible mode of the human heart is worship.[49] As the late novelist David Foster Wallace put it, "In the day-to-day trenches of adult life, there is no such thing as atheism. There is no such thing as not worshiping. Everybody worships. The only choice we get is what to worship."[50] It's not if you're worshiping; it's what you're worshiping. In the same way, it's not a question of whether cities are centers of worship—cities have always been built around the things that their inhabitants see as holding cosmic significance—it's a question of what a city is worshiping.

World-class cities are the largest religious communities in the world by virtue of their population density alone. And what do they tend to worship? People in cities "turn to false gods, such as power, fame, possessions, privilege, and comfort."[51] Consider the overarching cosmic narrative of Washington, DC: the pursuit of power. For the majority of the city's residents, daily life is shaped by power. Whether one is running for political office, holding the keys to history in a renowned museum, lobbying for a legislative shift, or maintaining and measuring military strength at the Pentagon, power is the name of the game. One might say that the order of life—the order of worship, or the urban liturgy—is determined by the "idol" of the city. This is true no matter what the idols of your city are. To adapt Greg Beale's thesis on idolatry, a city resembles what it reveres, either for ruin or for restoration.[52]

The idea of the city as a center for worship becomes complicated when we consider the overwhelming number of personal narratives that are weaved into a city's overarching story. Cities are centers of worship because they are filled to the brim with worshipers—people giving their lives away to realities they believe will fulfill them. Add to this the endless numbers of potential options for worship, and you find that city living has a unique way of fostering spiritual openness. "Cities tend to excite spiritual inquiry, both good and bad. The turmoil, the striving, and all that a city becomes seem to turn people into religious seekers."[53] Cities are centers of worship filled with people who worship, and all of these worshipers are very open to finding new objects to worship.

Some may find this spiritual openness threatening, but Christians ought to find it exciting. It is precisely this kind of urban spiritual seeking that provided the context for the rapid spread of the gospel in the first century. Craig Blomberg cites the following as a major factor in the quick advance of Christianity:

> A cosmopolitan spirit grew, particularly in the cities, that transcended national barriers. Old tribal distinctions and identities were breaking down, leaving people ripe for new religions or ideologies to fill the gaps. The gospel would meet many felt needs in this climate. . . . Closely related was the elimination of many cross-cultural barriers to dialogue and the dissemination of new worldviews.[54]

In this way, the global phenomenon of urbanization provides incredible opportunities for the spread and influence of the gospel that the church has not seen since its earliest days. The gospel is the one story that can rewrite all the misdirected stories that our cities are telling. It is *the* way that worship is rightly reordered and the way in which worship becomes life giving again. At bottom, the God of the gospel is who all worshipers are truly longing to find. Will they locate us, his people, in the city when they start searching for something to worship?

CONCLUSION

We hope that you'll be able to affirm that cities are important. An honest evaluation of past and present human experiences indicates that they are unmatched as centers of power, culture, and worship. In the future, these increasingly dense and numerous human settlements will lead, shape, and provide the narratives of purpose and meaning for our world. This is true regardless of whether one lives in the heart of a thriving metropolis or on the edge of a far-reaching exurban community. The looming challenge to all Christians will be whether we will bring the gospel to bear on these centers of influence, or simply react to the effects and overflow of the city. It is our contention that the gospel compels us not only to react, but more importantly to respond winsomely and to enter into the city's cultural story with a contextualized, renewing, and reviving power of the gospel. Before plotting our response, the next step is to determine just *why* it is that cities hold this place of immense influence in our world. After having examined the importance of cities, we move now to consider their characteristics.

DISCUSSION QUESTIONS

1. What preconceptions about the city did you bring with you into the first chapter of this book? How does your social location or personal background affect the way you view the city?
2. What is your gut-level reaction to the claim that our world will become increasingly urban in the years ahead? How would you deal with rapid urbanization if it reached your doorstep?

3. To what extent is it true that cities are centers of power? How often do you feel the effects of political and economic decisions that are made in cities?
4. Where do you see the direct impact of the city on your personal experience of culture? Media? Sports? A particular product? What are the implications of the urban background of the culture you consume?
5. What would it look like for your city to do away with its idols and turn to the one true God? How would your city be different if its inhabitants were driven by devotion to God rather than the selfish pursuit of wealth, fame, or power?

Chapter 2

THE
CHARACTERISTICS
OF CITIES

> Our cities' gleaming spires point to the greatness that
> mankind can achieve, but also to our hubris. . . . Urban in-
> novation can destroy value as well as create it.[1]
>
> **Edward Glaeser**

A WORLD ON THE MOVE

It is no secret that the twenty-first generation is more mobile than any generation that preceded it. Though current economic trends in the United States suggest that many people are choosing to "stay home,"[2] on the whole, the boundaries that held people in place for generations have now been removed. Mobility as we know and experience it began with the railroad, was expanded by the automobile and the advent of the airplane, and has been solidified through communication technologies like the telephone and the Internet. These developments have led to extreme changes in the way we think about place. Sociologist Richard Florida reflects:

> All these technologies have carried the promise of a boundless world. They would free us from geography, allowing us to move out of crowded cities and into lives of our own bucolic choosing. Forget the past, when cities and civilizations were confined to fertile soil, natural ports, or raw materials. In today's high-tech world, we are free to live wherever we want. Place, according to this increasingly popular view, is irrelevant.[3]

Thomas L. Friedman's wildly successful *The World Is Flat* went a long way in fixing the irrelevance of place in the mind of the average Westerner. We now dream of working from home, selling slices of our own perspective to like-minded isolated individuals across the globe. Stationed at a coffee shop, the imagined worker occasionally phones into an unknown office to report on video conference calls he has had with potential clients who happen to be planted in nondescript coffee shops around the world. We do not need place, and we certainly do not need cities, so the logic goes.

According to Florida, "It's a compelling notion, but it's wrong." As the previous chapter demonstrated, the phenomenon of urbanization is on the rise, is shaping our future, and happily, even if paradoxically, exists alongside the phenomenon of globalization. In a world where people have the ability to live and work wherever they would like, they are overwhelmingly choosing to live in densely populated cities.

In the first chapter, we essentially asked the question, *what* is a city? In seeking an answer, we found that cities are centers for power, culture, and worship. Our aim in this chapter is to answer the *why* questions. Why do cities function as centers for population and innovation? Why are cities uniquely suited to connect people across cultures and disciplines? And why is it that cities dominate the creative and economic landscape of our world? As we will see, it is the characteristics of cities as magnets (their ability to attract), amplifiers (their ability to turn up the volume), and engines (their ability to drive our world) that largely explain why they matter so greatly to our culture. We'll also find that it is these same characteristics that open up unprecedented opportunities for the spread of the gospel around the world.

THE CITY AS MAGNET

At this moment there are at least three types of people moving to the city nearest you. One could be a talented young musician. She was first violin in her competitive high school orchestra and now is looking to make an impression at the conservatory. On the same road you might find a man in his late thirties. He was uncomfortable in his hometown where he was marginalized on a number of different accounts: his race, economic status, style, and preference for what others often perceived as abnormal or unconventional. Finally, unsure of what he's getting himself into, a man who has lived in four different cities in the past four years crosses the city limits with the hopes of squeezing some life out of a new city, or at least indulging in the passions for the now.

Despite the differences that exist in their respective motivations, the common thread that holds all of these travelers together is their attraction to the city. It holds out promise, hope, and fulfillment in their pursuit of upward and social mobility. The city does not discriminate; it does not close its doors to any newcomers, but stands as a monument to possibility and potentiality. In this way, the city functions as a magnet. The following list represents the various types of individuals who are being drawn into cities.

The City as a Magnet for the Aspirational

Our first traveler is not unfamiliar with success. As we mentioned, she was the top violin player in her suburban high school orchestra, where she had opportunity to participate successfully in regional competitions. Graduating at the head of her class, she feels that she has earned her spot at the conservatory, and anticipates proving to her teachers and peers that she belongs at the top. Hard work got her here; hard work will define her while she is here. But why *here*? Why the city? One way to answer that question would be to name institutions, programs, teachers, orchestras, and so on. No matter the choice of discipline, you will find in cities the structures that produce the best, brightest, and most successful contributors to their respective industries. But the reason that an individual might be attracted to these structures runs much deeper than what is to be found on the surface. Cities contain large numbers of people who possess an abundance of that uniquely human trait known as aspiration.

This idea is best encapsulated in the closing stanza of Frank

Sinatra's "New York, New York." After singing the glories and opportunities of life in the city Sinatra proclaims, "And if I can make it there, I'm gonna make it anywhere." Like Sinatra, we know intuitively that cities are places where people go to prove themselves, to live out their dreams, achieve their highest desires, start new things, and advance their careers. This is why cities are packed with students, singles, young marrieds, entrepreneurs, high achievers, immigrants, and what has been termed the "creative class." Cities are talent magnets. If you want to make a name for yourself, there is no other place to do it than in the big city.

By no means does this nullify the fact that the city can be a difficult place for the aspirational. It's quite likely that our violinist will have her high hopes dashed the first time she enters a subway station and realizes that there are musicians who are more competent than she, busking for a few dollars an hour while being drowned out by passing trains. The star high school quarterback may sit on the bench at the university. The young restaurateur's first attempt at a gastropub may fall flat, leading to a retreat from the city. And for the aspirational individual, there is nothing worse than being ignored or going unnoticed. As William James once observed:

> No more fiendish punishment could be devised, were such a thing physically possible, than that one should be turned loose in society and remain absolutely unnoticed by all the members thereof. If no one turned around when we entered, answered when we spoke, or minded what we did, but if every person we met "cut us dead," and acted as if we were non-existent things, a kind of rage and impotent despair would before long well up in us, from which the cruelest bodily torture would be a relief.[4]

This is the dark side of urban aspiration. Even as it draws people, the city often isolates them. Success is promised but failure can follow. Though the city welcomes dreams, it can just as quickly crush those dreams. When seeking a name in the city, many will find out that they have no voice. In this way, the aspirational insecurities and idols are revealed. It is here that we find an entry point for the gospel, which claims that a name is something received, not earned. Aspirational people need to hear the good news of a God who can reshape hearts and identities from the inside out.

But the gospel is not only for aspirational people who will inevitably face difficult times, but also for marginalized people who are seeking to find refuge.

The City as a Magnet for the Marginalized

Second to be pulled into the city is the man who felt out of place and marginalized in his small town for a number of reasons, whether it be for his race, vocational choices, economic position, or lifestyle. For our purposes, this man represents any and all people who for one reason or another do not "fit" or are dissatisfied in a nonurban place. At the start, it should be noted that he is just as, if not more, aspirational than our first violinist. The lengths to which he is willing to go to bring about needed changes in his life place him squarely in the middle of our first category. This shows that there is inevitable overlap between the different groups of people. Nonetheless, to speak of the city as a "magnet for the marginalized" allows us to consider a large collection of individuals who have not yet been described in our discussion.

Marginalized people flock to cities because it is there that they find others who speak a common "language." Whether social, cultural, or actual, there are countless languages spoken in the city that are never experienced in suburban or rural areas. An individual who is an ethnic minority in a small town may only be able to speak her native language (both cultural and actual) to a few family members. It is likely that she will also experience heightened discrimination on the basis of her race.[5] In contrast, the city provides her an opportunity to surround herself with others who speak the same language. Simply put, the population density of cities allows the economically, socially, or culturally marginalized to craft places of refuge and safety that would ordinarily be out of reach in a small town.

Economic opportunity not only attracts aspirational professionals to the city, it also attracts the aspirational poor. For many readers, the urban core will be synonymous with poverty. As you've been reading about the importance of cities, you may even have found yourself asking, "Don't cities create and encourage serious cycles of poverty?" The question is a natural one as poverty is more readily visible in cities than in the suburbs. Interestingly enough though, this is another place where the aspirational and the dissatisfied overlap. According to Glaeser, "Cities aren't full of poor people because cities make people poor, but because cities *attract* poor people with the prospect of improving their lot in life." As a result, "we should worry more about places with too little poverty. Why do they fail to attract the least fortunate?"[6] The city is a magnet for the economically dissatisfied because, of all potential locations, it holds out the greatest opportunities for advancement. The concentration of the poor in cities is also a significant reason for gospel-driven Christians to consider seeking out new ways to serve the city.[7]

Social factors also send people running to urban areas. Usually more tolerant and open-minded than their suburban counterparts, cities attract marginalized artists who lack a hearing for their work in small-town settings. It is also well documented that cities tend to contain a higher concentration of homosexuals than rural regions.[8] In providing a haven for these and other socially marginalized individuals, cities continue to fulfill their historical role as places of safety and refuge.[9]

The flip side of the city's promise of economic prosperity and social tolerance is the dissatisfaction we all eventually find in unfulfilled promises. Many will never earn enough money to move beyond the life of economic disadvantage that drove them to the city. Many cities do not have the necessary systems in place to move individuals from poverty to prosperity. Tolerance, when taken to the extreme, has often led to significant societal degeneration.[10] Though the city holds tremendous possibility for the marginalized, in and of itself, it will never fully satisfy.

The City as Magnet for the Explorational

This third category is a bit smaller, and is also the hardest to pin down. However, it is useful insofar as it brings into focus a group of individuals that may not quite identify as being aspirational or marginalized. Here we mainly have in view the aforementioned explorational artist and his friends. Creatives, nonconformists, escapists, free spirits—many people are flocking to cities in search of new experiences and a fresh start.

The heterogeneous nature of cities, over against the more homogeneous tendencies of suburban living, makes urban centers ideal places for the adventurous, the wandering, and the avant-garde. Cities are more friendly to the "morally relativist, urban-oriented, culturally adventurous, [and] sexually polymorphist" than are traditional suburban communities.[11] Taking advantage of a higher threshold for unorthodox approaches to life, nonconforming individuals migrate to cities to experience "the new" and carve out an identity that might be less acceptable or misunderstood in a small town or rural area. "Individuality, self-expression and openness to difference are favored over . . . homogeneity, conformity and 'fitting in.'"[12]

As we will see later in this chapter, cities and cultures often benefit greatly from these risk-taking creatives and explorationists. However, without fail, the cities of this world will fail to satiate the original explorational longings that lead to urban migration. There is no pluralistic environment, no combination of experiences, no forged identity robust enough to bring deep and enduring satisfaction to the explorational individual. Unique to Christianity, the claim that there is a coming city in which the explorationist will find permanent fulfillment opens wide new doors for potential gospel proclamation.

If we now know a bit more about the magnetic quality of cities, can anything be said about the conditions that are necessary for the thriving that so often takes place within them?

THE CITY AS AMPLIFIER

No matter from what angle we look at the city, we must admit: re-markable things happen when diverse groupings of aspirational, marginalized, and explorational people end up living and working in close proximity to one another. The strength of any given city lies in its ability to capitalize population density by fostering connectivity across diverse social, ideological, and professional lines. World-class cities function as amplifiers for the skills, talents, and ideas of their citizens. They do this by understanding and taking advantage of the interplay between two uniquely urban phenomena: clustered density and connective diversity.

Clustered Density

Consider the fact that 42 percent of New York State's population chooses to live in New York City. At just 305 square miles, the city accounts for only .006 percent of the state's land. That so many people choose to pay often exorbitant costs to call that city home is a testa-ment that unique things are happening on the relatively small patches of space that house the world's cities. But what exactly happens when people cluster together in cities? Is population density a problem that needs to be addressed? Or is it an asset that needs to be leveraged?

For many people, the density of cities is actually fear inducing. The thought of packed subway cars and overcrowded apartment com-plexes has led many to view the city as an essentially volatile, unsafe environment.[13] However, the growing human consensus seems to be that cities, despite their sometimes-crowded nature, are increasingly preferable to rural and suburban human settlements. Why?

The primary reason why we choose to live in close proximity to one another is that regular, challenging face-to-face interactions with other people make us more creative, innovative, and productive.

Ingenuity and imagination are amplified by way of interaction. At least part of what makes us uniquely human is our ability to connect with one another, and we do that more often in cities than in any other setting.[14] Glaeser has said that we are "machines for learning from the people next to us."[15] This means that despite, or perhaps in light of, our increasingly technologized world, cities have become more important than ever before. Nowhere are more people more "next to us" than in the city.

You know what it is like to share an idea with friends or coworkers, and to receive their critique and refinement. If you are around people who are genuinely interested in ideas and who have a creative impulse, then you soon find out that your idea is better than it was at the start. We might say that the power of the idea is in the sharing. This often occurs in the world of writing. In the case of *Why Cities Matter*, we both had a desire to write about the city, but believed that we could write a better book together than we might separately. Furthermore, we decided to have friends and editors take a look at the manuscript. Thanks to this process, it's our belief that the book you hold in your hands is better than the one you would be reading if Stephen or Justin had written the entire volume without outside input.

In cities, this kind of sharing and sharpening happens daily, across all industries and fields. It is in dense urban environments that the individual and corporate potential for thinking, creating, working, and producing is maximized. It is what one urbanist has called "the clustering force."[16] When my idea bumps up against your idea, the effect is one of both amplification and multiplication; our individual approaches are strengthened, while new ideas are spawned. Add the element of competition, and you have a recipe for extraordinary development and growth. Admittedly, conflict is often a by-product of this creative exchange, but it is this very by-product that can provide an opportunity for the development of human empathy alongside creative production. Clustered talent in dense cities produces innovation.[17]

Connective Diversity[18]

What about cities that don't display the qualities of amplification and multiplication? One could easily point to a city like Detroit, which presently seems to lack the creative energy discussed above, as a counterexample.[19] Knowing that the Motor City does not stand alone as a struggling city, have we overstated our case for the power of clustered density to amplify human inventiveness? What do industrial cities in the United States's Rust Belt lack that has made their coastal rivals such vital players on the global level?

The one phenomenon guaranteed to stifle the power of density is homogeneity. In other words, if everyone in a city does the same thing for work, thinks along the same lines, and lives relatively similar lives, no matter how densely clustered they may be, that city will lack the necessary innovational capital needed to sustain itself over the long haul. So, for instance, the traditional manufacturing city, with factories at its center, has density—yes. But with a dependence on a single industry that requires only labor of its employees, it is only a matter of time before the bottom falls out. The result is that many leave the city for jobs elsewhere, and those who remain lack both jobs and the necessary skills to build for the future. In no way is this meant to isolate manufacturing as an unimportant or inadequate industry; the same could be said of finance, academia, service, etc. If a densely populated city lacks diversity of human capital, its inevitable long-term result will be decline. Urbanist Jane Jacobs summarized it best in the concluding words of her classic work on cities: "Lively, diverse, intense cities contain the seeds of their own regeneration, with energy enough to carry over for problems and needs outside themselves."[20]

Density minus Diversity equals Addition. A city can be extremely large, but if its inhabitants are largely homogeneous, the addition of new inhabitants is just that: addition. Population growth does not coincide with economic, innovational, or infrastructural growth.

Density plus Diversity equals Multiplication. Even if the city itself is not huge, if its inhabitants are diverse in their thinking, work, and living, the result is multiplication. Ideas, industries, and institutions will all proliferate.

When the bottom falls out on a *density-minus-diversity* city, population addition becomes subtraction, and there is no platform left on which to rebuild. On the contrary, when things begin to head south in a *density-plus-diversity* city, population subtraction is counteracted by multiplication. In other words, a diversity of people, ideas, thoughts, industries, and new ventures is the capital upon which thriving cities are built and sustained. To push the amplifier metaphor a bit further, density is the power switch and diversity is the volume knob. All the potential for significant output is present in the dense population clusters that are our cities. Diversity is the means by which the volume is turned up and the potential begins to be loudly realized.

The effects of diversity are often more recognizable on a person-to-person level. Sure, it is great to be around people who are *like* us, but there is a certain kind of growth and sharpening that can take place only when we spend time with people who are *unlike* us.[21] For example, to paint with a broad brush, there are certain cultural presuppositions held by Westerners that are not shared by Easterners. Typically, the West has placed a premium on the autonomous individual, while the East has favored corporate solidarity. If a Westerner lacks meaningful, personal access to viewpoints apart from his own, it will be quite easily assumed that self-sovereignty is not only the norm, but also the correct way of understanding his relationship to others. Obviously, the reverse could be said of the Easterner.

In contrast to settings that tend to move toward homogeneity, most cities provide us opportunities to live in close proximity to a variety of people who are *unlike* us. Musicians interact with engineers. Tech developers mix with professors of American history. Scientists bump into theologians. Easterners cross paths with Westerners. This is not to say that urbanites always capitalize on these interactions. In fact, cities can sometimes be places of isolation and even segregation. Nonetheless, the opportunity for diverse interaction is present in cities, even if city dwellers do not always take advantage of it. In most ex-urban and rural communities, diverse exchanges and relationships are often not even an option, most certainly not at the level at which they are available in urban centers.

In short, the potentially powerful effects of clustered density are dependent upon a city's track record of fostering connective diversity. When these two aspects of a city interact, the result is the amplification of human potential in every dimension of life and culture. When cities thrive at amplifying their citizens' talents, skills, and ideas, they become the engines that drive our world, for good or for ill.

THE CITY AS ENGINE

What happens when aspirational, marginalized, and explorational people cluster into densely packed, diverse cities? When the volume gets turned up on human ingenuity and invention, what is the result? We would like to suggest that cities, when thriving, act as engines that capitalize on amplified human resources in order to drive our world. As magnets, cities attract all types of people. As amplifiers, they provide an environment for the flourishing and sharpening of their citizens. As engines, cities take the collective talents, skills, and creativity of their citizens and translate them into world-driving technology, industry, and cultural development. In what follows, we consider how the urban engine runs, as well as where it often ends up taking us.

Fuel: Creativity

As we've already stated, nowhere else do ideas, innovation, and industries collide like they do in the world's finest cities. The city has always been a place ripe for change and development, and this is increasingly the case in our present day. While the explosive growth of many cities in the nineteenth century was tied to the gains of the Industrial Revolution, today's rapid and global urbanization is tied to a new currency: creativity. As many have noted, our world is no longer animated by the manufacturing of goods; it is now propelled by ideas.[22]

Creativity is the fuel on which the world increasingly runs. And nowhere is this fuel to be found in greater abundance than in cities. In "The Geography of Creativity," a landmark study on the location of innovation in Great Britain, researchers found that in nearly every case, the dense clustering of creativity overlapped with the population density found in Britain's cities. Perhaps unsurprisingly, one city was found to hold "pre-eminence as . . . Britain's creative powerhouse": London. Not only does London hold this general predominance, it also has a particular hold on high-level creative sectors. "London specialises in the most creative activities of the value chain of all sectors. . . . Although high levels of creative agglomeration can be found in other regions . . . they tend to be associated with functions down the creative value chain. . . . London has a 'stronger creative intensity' (this is, that a higher proportion of creative professionals working in what we would define as purely 'creative activities') than other places in Great Britain."[23]

What is true in Great Britain is true across the board. Evidence shows that rather than living in Friedman's "flat world," we actually live in what Florida has labeled a "spiky world."[24] A spiky world is one in which people, money, and other resources crowd together in cities, and the most dramatically and densely clustered commodity is innovation. How concentrated are the creatives and their ideas? Venture capital firms (i.e., those who invest money in ideas, technologies, etc.), all of which cluster in cities, are known for invoking the "twenty-minute rule": "only companies within a twenty-minute commute of the VC firm's office are considered worthy of a high-risk investment."[25]

Ideas outside of this radius are hardly considered. With serious money on the line, why would a VC firm limit itself to ideas within twenty minutes of the city? They are banking on the fact that if an idea is worth hearing, worth investing in, it will make it to the city. If you're drilling for creativity—the fuel on which the urban engine runs—go to the city.

"OK," you say. "Creativity is the key, and it's usually found in cities, but what makes urban ideas uniquely potent and powerful?"

Function: Competition

Hit the gas pedal in your car and the engine under the hood will turn the fuel into energy. The engine functions to convert gas into motion. In the urban engine, the fuel of creativity is put into motion by competition. Competition takes creativity to the next level and explains, in large part, the concentration of cultural capital in cities.

Consider the average small town. With one fancy restaurant, one school, one computer repair shop, one grocery store, and a host of other singular entities, the town provides its citizens with much of what they need for daily living. As it stands, this town is a wonderful place to live, and it may even have some of the creative fuel about which we've been speaking. What it lacks, however, is competition—something that cities have in droves. The aforementioned grocery store has acted as the town's food supplier for more than thirty years. From one angle, this is a community stabilizer. From another, we might honestly be able to assess the store as somewhat outdated and quite limited in its inventory. With little to no competition over its significant tenure, the store has settled into a routine, and the tastes of the townspeople have grown accustomed to what the store provides. Sadly, this store could be easily knocked out of its preeminent position in the community if a big-box store were to come to town with affordable variety.

The story is different in cities where the creativity of a clustered and heterogeneous population leads to fruitful competition. Urban diversity demands variety, and urban density is able to support it. Firms, hospitals, restaurants, museums, and more all rise to the challenge and compete with one another to serve best the needs of the urban community. And, believe it or not, the leaders in every field understand that this competition is a *benefit*, not an obstacle. "When people—especially talented and creative ones—come together, ideas flow more freely, and as a result individual and aggregate talents increase exponentially: the end result amounts to much more than the sum of its parts."[26] One end result is that "Americans who live in metropolitan areas with more than a million residents are, on average, 50 percent more productive than Americans who live in smaller metropolitan areas."[27] This, in turn, is accompanied by higher wages. So, more often than not, the competition of creative and skilled people in cities benefits all involved parties. The creative friction that is present in cities is the mechanism that turns the fuel of creativity into cultural forward momentum. But what is the end result? Haven't cities and the creative people in them often pushed our world in the wrong direction? Or does the city actually give us glimpses of what a flourishing humanity might look like?

Fruit: Culmination (Flourishing or Famishing)

In recent years, secular urbanists have made significant claims about the benefits of city living. The subtitle of Edward Glaeser's *Triumph of the City* is a snapshot of an increasingly common urban optimism: *How Our Greatest Invention Makes Us Richer, Smarter, Greener, Healthier, and Happier.* Others add to this positive perspective by claiming that the city is the answer to our world's growing ecological woes.[28] In some cases, the discussion takes on a nearly religious tone—cities themselves are our future, our hope. We are entering "a new golden age of the city."[29] It is thought that if you simply move to the right city you can "maximize your chances for a happy and fulfilling life."[30] Admittedly, this hopeful tone stands in contrast to the more measured approach of the notable urbanists of the mid to late twentieth century. In their respective classics on the city, both Lewis Mumford and Jane Jacobs expressed a great love for the city while maintaining a reasonable amount of suspicion about the city's ability to fulfill its promises to humanity.[31]

The high-flung claims of the new urbanist raise the question of what a city is capable of doing for its inhabitants. As we bring this chapter toward its close, we want to suggest the following answer to that question. While our earthly cities can never provide ultimate refuge, fulfillment, or hope to their citizens, by God's common grace they can flourish humanity and foreshadow that future city in which we will ultimately thrive in perfect communion with our God.

With this in mind, we can see that the optimism of the new urbanist is based in part on the reality that cities *are* ideal places for human flourishing. We see this in the Psalms where the creational language of flourishing ("springs of water"; "fruitful yield"; "multiply greatly") is connected with an earthly city that the Lord provides for his people (107:4–9, 35–38). The prophet Jeremiah is unafraid to connect the flourishing of an exiled people with the well-being of a pagan city ("in its welfare you will find your welfare," Jer. 29:7). In the same way, we can look at the welfare of our present-day cities and find both the blessing of God's common grace and the foreshadowing of the promised final city.

As places of remarkable creativity and competition, our cities have the ability to drive us to new heights of ingenuity and invention. To study the history and present state of the world's great cities "is to study nothing less than human progress."[32] We should be eager to celebrate all the blessings that are found in our cities. Where truth, goodness, and beauty are the result of the urban engine, Christians ought to lead the way in pointing out the grace of God at work. In this way, the city offers us countless opportunities rightly to direct our worship to the one true God. Additionally, as we will see in the pages to come, Christians ought also to be the ones striving toward this truth, goodness, and beauty—the common good—as those who desire to cause the entire city to rejoice (Prov. 11:10).[33]

And yet, we have suggested that our cities cannot fulfill us in any ultimate sense. Indeed, they are cracked and broken, unable to sustain the weight of our worship. It is often the case that the urban engine creates more cultural "pollution" than it does true prosperity. "Our cities' gleaming spires point to the greatness that mankind can achieve, but also to our hubris."[34] Cities have the potential to be engines for human flourishing, but when they interact with human sinfulness, they can become centers of injustice, indulgence, and idolatry. Philip Bess offers a balanced perspective: "There's a reciprocal relationship between good cities and human flourishing. Good cities make it possible for us to live better than if we lived without cities. Nevertheless, even the best city can't make a person good, can't make a person happy."[35]

As engines for the production of culture, our cities have the ability either to lead us to human flourishing or to human famishing. In the end, the question is one of worship. When the citizens of a city are animated by a loving response to the grace of God, the city will flourish and rejoice. When urban dwellers run on self-interest, self-indulgence, and self-definition, the city will eventually turn in on itself and wither. If in the end the well-being of a city is tied to what it worships, might this provide a significant entry point for the gospel in an increasingly urban world?

THE CITY AS GOSPEL GATEWAY

There is a great deal more to be said about urbanization and the nature of cities. By no means have we exhausted the subject, nor have we offered a definitive treatment. The interested reader will find countless articles and books on the topic.[36] We have even provided a list of some of the best of these resources at the close of this book. But, being church planters and pastors who know personally the transforming power of the gospel, our interest in the topic is much more than to understand the historical, sociocultural, and economic dimensions of the city. In light of all we've covered to this point, we want to ask, "Does rapid global urbanization, the nature of cities, and the growing influence of cities on our world provide us with a challenge, opportunity, and mandate for gospel-centered Christians in the twenty-first century and beyond?" Knowing what we know—that our world is growing increasingly urban, that cities are magnets for spiritually curious people, that cities set our world's cultural and liturgical agenda—should the shape of Christian ministry and cultural engagement in our day have a strategically urban focus? How should Christians concerned for the spread and impact of the gospel relate to the cities of the world?

Starting with a look at the Bible's approach to the city in the next chapter, we will argue throughout the rest of this book that the gospel not only encourages but also uniquely equips us to respond to urbanization and all that it entails. Cities are important, yes; but they along with their citizens are also fallen and broken, and in need of the renewing and reconciling grace of God in Christ (Rom. 8:19–21; Col. 1:20). It is ultimately the upside-down, power-sharing, worship-reordering, redemptive work of Christ that urban dwellers lack and need. It is this deficit that drives idolatrous aspirations toward wealth, power, and comfort, along with untethered, selfish expressions of explorationism. It is humanity's abuse of God-given resources and creativity that has led to marginalizing inequalities and social injustices. Though God has gifted our cities with creative and competitive people, so often the fruit of our labors is self-centeredness and overconsumption, rather than a worshipful spirit that leads to human flourishing.

We believe that the very real needs of the city are answered most holistically by God's redemptive plan for this world as it is laid out in Scripture. Only the gospel can ultimately meet the needs of our cities. It may be the case that the church—we who are called to herald and be shaped by the good news—is on the verge of participating in a significant movement of the gospel in the cities of the world. As we consider this exciting possibility, there is no better place to begin than with the Bible's perspective on cities.

DISCUSSION QUESTIONS

1. Why do you think that some individuals are magnetically drawn to the city, while others are seemingly repelled by it? How would you explain the recently intensified migration to cities?
2. Cities are tightly packed, noisy places. What are some of the benefits of clustered density? How would living in closer proximity to your neighbor change the way that you seek to share the gospel with them?
3. Why do humans thrive when they live with people who are both like and unlike them? To which group do you tend to gravitate?

Think of a time when you grew in your knowledge and experience of the gospel because you came into contact with someone who was unlike you.

4. If cities are really the engines that drive our world, what do you make of the direction in which they have driven us to this point? Are cities living up to their promise? Do you see more signs of hope or despair in your city?

5. Does rapid global urbanization and the growing influence of cities provide gospel-centered Christians with a challenge, opportunity, and mandate for mission and ministry? Is it a far-fetched idea to think that cities around the world might increasingly serve as gateways and entry points for the gospel?

Chapter 3

THE BIBLE AND THE CITY

The New Jerusalem . . . is the Garden of Eden, remade. The City is the fulfilment of the purposes of the Eden of God. We began in a garden but will end in a city; God's purpose for humanity is urban![1]

Timothy Keller

We often undervalue the environment in which we live. We might appreciate our employment and our friends who live in the city, but we sometimes devalue our neighborhoods and fail to recognize that the Bible views places, such as cities, to be sacred. Place matters. "Place is a quintessentially human concept."[2] Author Edward Casey clarifies this description of being-in-place by saying that "to exist at all . . . is to have a place—to be implaced, however minimally or temporarily."[3] A brief survey of the importance of a place, such as cities, in the Bible's story line will help us to understand God's strategic inclusion of cities in his redemptive plan.

THE CITY IN THE OLD TESTAMENT

The Garden City in Genesis

City building was prized in the ancient Near Eastern world. In the Bible, the building of cities was associated with order, stewardship, cultivating the earth's riches and resources, and bearing God's image in the world through the creation of life and beauty. The cultivation of a place for production first started when God asked Adam and Eve to carry out the cultural mandate—to subdue and rule the earth (Gen. 1:28). Norbert Lohfink argues that "to subdue" the earth "refers not to wanton destruction but to multiplication and expansion over the earth."[4] God called Adam and Eve to steward the earth's resources and to cultivate and develop their use in the garden, by harnessing their powers in order to produce agriculture, architecture, the arts, science, family life, business, and commerce, and to develop a God-honoring civilization under God's reign.[5] For humanity to be implaced in the landscape of Eden shows that place matters to God, and the "interplay between humans and their contexts means that place has a developmental, cultural dimension."[6] Since a sense of place is a human hunger and nothing we do is unplaced,[7] God implaced humanity into a garden with all the raw materials for culture making and place making so that they would not become placeless but rooted.

Gordon Wenham suggests that it is hard to be certain whether the ancient Near Eastern background is informing Genesis 2, but gardens in Mesopotamia and Egypt were often described as expansive urban parks and not undeveloped wildernesses.[8] Bartholomew builds this argument by saying, "What is clear on all accounts is that a garden was an enclosed area designed for cultivation . . . [so] what we have, then, rather than an image of primitivism, is one of an area that is bounded, probably by walls; carefully landscaped; intensively cultivated with orchards and the like. In the light of its urban connotations in the ancient Near East, Eden may well have included buildings."[9] Although this interpretation might seem extremely creative and imaginative, Meredith Kline agrees that the development of culture is grounded in city building and cultivation. In this sense, God is the ultimate, creative, entrepreneurial urban planter who is also a cosmically implaced coinhabitant of this garden city.

Therefore, the images of the garden in Genesis become urban images in the rest of Scripture.[10] The psalmist alludes to the river in the garden (Gen. 2:10) when he declares that "there is a river whose streams make glad the city of God, the holy habitation of the Most High" (Ps. 46:4). This Edenic image is picked up in Zechariah 14:8, where it portrays a day when the "living waters shall flow out from Jerusalem." These rivers, waters, streams, and bubbling springs, which represent a special symbol for life, describe a future paradisal garden of complete restoration. The two garden items, namely the river and the tree of life, are prominently featured in the holy city, the New Jerusalem coming down from heaven (Rev. 21:2).

This divine call for humanity was, ultimately, an urban mandate. One of the first achievements of this enduring mandate was the expansion of the borders of the garden, the construction of a city (Gen. 4:17). Adam and Eve launched not only the history of humanity and the family, but also the history of cities and culture.

Life in the garden was always intended to grow into life in the city. "The couple in the garden was to multiply, so providing the citizens of the city. Their cultivation of earth's resources as they extended their control over their territorial environment through the fabrication of sheltering structures would produce the physical architecture of the city."[11] The city is a larger version of the life, work, and relationships found in the garden. The DNA of the human family engaged in orderly cultural production (subduing and ruling the earth) was to become the DNA of the city—multiplied humanity doing life together in the city, under God. Simply put, "the city is mankind culturally formed."[12]

God created humanity to be his representatives, to be his estate managers—to draw out and steward the resources of the earth, to build its culture and civilization. Just like God, as image bearers of God, humans are commissioned to bring order out of chaos,[13] to take the raw ingredients of the garden and to develop them into something that causes life to flourish and God to be glorified. Adam and Eve were created in God's image to reflect the creative, entrepreneurial activity of God in order to create culture from the raw materials given by God.[14] God designed the city with purpose and power. The city is the place that brings together and focuses human capacity to steward the resources of the earth in order to build its culture and civilization. This was God's original cosmic plan for his creation. Did humanity's fall change God's plans and concerns for the city?

Many discussions of the Bible's perspective on the city begin in

Genesis 4. After having murdered his brother Abel (v. 8), Cain leaves God's presence and settles "east of Eden" (v. 16). There, we learn that "he built a city" and named it after his son (v. 17). This is the first explicit reference to the city in the Bible, and because Cain is cast as a shadowy character throughout the scriptural narrative, many have assumed that his shadow falls on the city. However, rather than being "an act of self-aggrandizement, . . . the very act of constituting this city is the fruition of Cain's own search for security in the world."[15] In other words, Cain builds a city for the same reason that God will later instruct Israel to build cities, namely, as places of refuge and safety for sinners and murderers (Numbers 35; Joshua 20). Even in the midst of Cain's self-interested city building, God's design for cities as places of refuge is being carried out. Though humanity is fallen as a result of sin, the city retains at least a hint of the benefits and blessing it was intended to hold for humanity.

In this way, Kline argues for the goodness of the city despite the effects of sin on God's urban intentions:

> The city is not to be regarded as an evil invention of . . . fallen man. . . . The ultimate goal set before humanity at the very beginning was that human culture should take city-form. . . . There should be an urban structuring of human historical existence. . . . The cultural mandate given at creation was a mandate to build the city. Now, after the fall, the city is still a benefit, serving humankind as refuge from the howling wilderness condition into which the fallen human race, exiled from paradise, has been driven. . . . The common grace city has remedial benefits even in a fallen world. It becomes the drawing together of resources, strength, and talent no longer just for mutual complementation in the task of developing the resources of the created world, but now a pooling of power for defense against attack, and as an administrative community of welfare for the relief of those destitute by reason of the cursing of the ground.[16]

The city derives its legitimacy and purpose from God. God is the one who commissioned and empowered humanity to "be fruitful," to "multiply," to "fill the earth," to "subdue" and "have dominion" over "all the earth" (Gen. 1:28–29). "In the creation that God established there is one city to be built. That city will extend the glory of God throughout the earth. [With the fall,] humanity exercises autonomy, wresting the city from divine service and to self-glorification."[17] Nonetheless, the second chapter of the Bible shows God's original intent to expand humanity's borders and establish new urban settlements, an intent that remains unchanged by the shadow of rebellion and curse.[18]

Chapters later, Genesis 11 describes a population that had no interest in serving as city builders for God and as a God-honoring society, but who instead built for themselves "a city and tower with its top in the heavens" in order to "make a name" for themselves (v. 4). Despite the sinful city building we often see both in the Bible and in our world, the city gets its power from God. God invented the city. "Indeed, the only reason that cities have the power for evil that they do is because they were given culture-forming power by God. What makes them evil is not their city-ness, but the purpose to which they are put."[19]

Human history is moving forward in the direction of a city. The history of the world and the history of redemption converge, climax, and center on a bustling city. The last two chapters of the Bible reveal that the new heavens and the new earth will take the form of a city, and it will one day be inhabited by God's people. "Then I saw a new heaven and a new earth, for the first heaven and the first earth had passed away. . . . And I saw the holy city, new Jerusalem, coming down out of heaven from God. . . . And I heard a loud voice from the throne saying, 'Behold, the dwelling place of God is with man'" (Rev. 21:1–3).

This city will be a restored and more developed version of God's original creation. Two prominent riches in the garden of Eden, the river of life (Gen. 2:10) and the tree of life (Gen. 2:9), take center stage in the renewed garden city of the New Jerusalem: "Then the angel showed me *the river of the water of life*, bright as crystal, flowing from the throne of God and of the Lamb through the middle of the street of the city; also, on either side of the river, *the tree of life* with its twelve kinds of fruit, yielding its fruit each month" (Rev. 22:1–2). Harvie Conn comments:

> The city is the fulfillment of the purposes of the Eden of God . . . the city is the fulfiller of the paradise of God . . . which is tied to the future city with the original, sinless past of Eden and its restoration in Christ. Even under the curse, man's cultural calling will be maintained.[20]

If Adam had not sinned in the garden, he would have cultivated all the cultural riches of God's creation and developed it (eventually) into a perfect eternal city as described in Revelation 21–22. The garden of Eden is an introductory picture of what a great city like New York, San Francisco, or London could look like without the effects of human sin and rebellion.

City building is not an accidental sociological development. City building is God's idea, invention, and intention.

The Promised Land and Settlement in Canaan

The word for "city" in the Old Testament is used to refer to a wide range of settlements, from large cities ruled by a king to smaller towns or villages that were dependent on a major nearby city for protection and commerce. The importance of a city was not measured by its size, but by the strength of the city's fortification (its walls and gates) and by the services of protection, oversight of civil law, and the administration of political order and public affairs for inhabitants in its surrounding territories.

Although Cain built his city for self-protection, God's intention was to develop cities as places of refuge where urban settlers could receive divine protection. The Bible repeatedly describes the city as a place of "refuge" (Num. 35:25, 27; 20:4; 21:13; Judg. 9:35). The Israelites understood this important aspect of cities even in the years before they settled into the Promised Land. In fact, there is reason to believe that the Israelites considered themselves an urban people traveling toward a new city, rather than as an ideally nomadic popula-tion.[21] Their journey toward a new city approached culmination when God instructed the Israelites to settle in Canaan. There, they were to build cities and use them as places where God's people would be able to find life, compassion, and justice. Less populous, unwalled, nonur-ban dwelling places provided little defense against enemies, injustice, and unpredictable agricultural cycles. Cities provided refuge and op-portunity that could not be found elsewhere. Such cities were meant to model the secure, corporate life God wanted his people to have—to be centers of rightly ordered worship of the one true God.

Jerusalem, David's Kingdom, and the City Psalms

King David selected Jerusalem, a centrally situated city, to serve as Israel's capital (2 Sam. 5:9). David developed Jerusalem as the geo-graphic center of Israel's worship (2 Sam. 6:12–15; 15:29) and the capital location for political, cultural, and commercial life. Jerusalem was established as "the city of David" (2 Sam. 5:7; 6:10) but more im-portantly theologically, it became known as the city of God (1 Kings 11:36; 14:21; 2 Kings 21:4; Neh. 11:1). The Bible refers to Jerusalem simply as "the city" in Ezekiel 7:23, and as the supreme God-chosen city in the "City Psalms" (Pss. 46:4; 48:1–2, 8; 87:1–3; 122:3; 127:1). This city of peace, which reflects the garden city in Eden with the centralized locus of God's presence, is also a model of the future New Jerusalem, which stands at the center of the world with the temple of God built on top of the city. Unlike the skyscraper of the city of Babel, which stood as a monument to human pride, the temple in Jerusalem stood as a skyscraper and tribute to the King of the city who was bring-ing joy to a whole new urban society (Ps. 48:2), whose foundations are glorious (Psalm 87). Every Israelite knew where to find his God. God could be found in his holy city, Jerusalem, where his temple stood. Later, those who were removed from Jerusalem in the exile would re-peatedly express their longing to be with God again by returning to the city where God is enthroned (Pss. 46:4–5; 107:4, 7, 36). Even as

Adam and Eve longed to return to the garden, here we see that being in a city where the presence of God dwells has always been an essential human desire.

The psalmist is reminding the reader that God can be found primarily in the city because he dwells in the holy place. These texts paint a portrait of God as the ultimate urban dweller: "There is a river whose streams make glad the city of God, the holy habitation of the Most High" (Ps. 46:4; cf. Ps. 48:1); God is a lover of the city, he is concerned about its welfare: "She will not fall; God will help her at break of day" (Ps. 46:5 NIV). The psalmist's message of hope to God's people in Psalm 48 is for them to know that God is deeply concerned about his holy city and its inhabitants, and that he will continue to love, protect, bless, build, and invest all of himself in the preservation and expansion of the city, "as we have heard, so have we seen in the city of the LORD Almighty, in the city of our God: God makes her secure forever. . . . Walk about Zion, go around her, count her towers, consider well her ramparts, view her citadels, that you may tell of them to the next generation" (Ps. 48:8, 12–13 NIV). Even the nearby villages and suburban towns are glad because of the prosperity of the city: "The villages of Judah are glad because of your judgments" (v. 11 NIV). People were being asked to walk around the streets of Jerusalem marveling at the beauty of God's architecture, the detailing of all the various structures of the city, and proclaiming to everyone and to the next generation that God made all of this, and that he loves it, and that he is eternally committed to the city. The repeated refrain is that the city should be celebrated and God's people should hope for a transformed community.

The Exile

Several passages in the Prophetic writings further expose both God's love for the city and the mission he gives his people for the city. God declares that though the city has been abandoned and rejected, he will renew and rebuild it into a shining testimony of God's renown: "Although you [the city of the Lord] have been forsaken and hated . . .

I will make you the everlasting pride and the joy of all generations," a redeemed city existing "for the display of my splendor" (Isa. 60:15, 21 NIV).

In another remarkable biblical story, God shows his love not only for his own holy city, Jerusalem, but also for a notoriously pagan city, Nineveh. Although the prophet Jonah ran away from his missional call to preach against the wickedness of the Ninevites, God expressed his love for this city in a stunning statement: "You have been concerned about this vine, though you did not tend it or make it grow. . . . But Nineveh has more than a hundred and twenty thousand people who cannot tell their right hand from their left, and many cattle as well. Should I not be concerned about that great city?" (Jonah 4:10–11 NIV). Nineveh was a densely settled city that was full of worshipers who could not "tell their right hand from their left." There was potential there for great worship of the one true God—an opportunity to transform a city's pluralistic idolatry into monotheistic devotion. Amazingly, in calling Nineveh to repentance and reordering their worship, God shows that he loved Nineveh just as he had loved Jerusalem!

Jeremiah 28–29 describes a time in Israel when the professional leaders were taken into captivity by the Babylonian Empire. This elite group of Israelites needed to determine what sort of cultural posture they would take, whether they would separate themselves completely or assimilate and become utterly Babylonized. Living in exile, they believed they had only two options in relating to Babylon. The Babylonians wanted the Israelites to accommodate completely to their cultural, political, and religious landscape so that they would lose their distinct spiritual identity as the people of God. The false prophets of Israel (Jer. 29:8–9), on the other hand, were directing the people to stay completely out of the city of Babylon in order to preserve their unique identity and heritage. But Jeremiah pointed the people toward an unexplored third option when he spoke God's words: "Build houses and settle down; plant gardens and eat what they produce. Marry and have sons and daughters. . . . Increase in number there; . . . Also, seek the peace and prosperity of the city to which I have carried you into exile. Pray to the LORD for it, because if it prospers, you too will prosper . . . [I have] plans to give you hope and a future" (Jer. 29:5–7, 11 NIV). God provided a different option for city life than did the Babylonians and the false prophets. God called his people to seek the prosperity of the city—to live as a culturally distinct people in the heart of the city, responding to the surprising call to be salt and light and pursuing the common good by being the best citizens of their respective earthly cities.[22]

INTERLUDE: BETWEEN THE TESTAMENTS

God's call for his people to be his representatives who would embody a faithful presence in Babylon was filled with great promise. But history bears out that Israel would falter yet again in its attempt to carry out this mandate. Though God had been gracious to sustain and renew Israel's missional calling *even* while sending them into exile, true to form, they would fail to live faithfully as God's people. Yes, eventually they would return to Jerusalem, rebuild the temple, and even reconstruct city walls, but questions would remain unanswered throughout the intertestamental period. The silent years in which God would send no new prophets and confirm no new promises effectively created an atmosphere of uncertainty and insecurity.

In exile, Israel had been removed from God's chosen city of refuge. Designed as a place of divinely preserved safety, Jerusalem itself no longer provided protection for God's wayward people. In the heart of what they had come to know as enemy territory, the idea of the city was no longer a comforting security. Outside of Jerusalem, Israel was effectively a shelterless people. Once released from exile, the Jerusalem they would return to was one governed by foreign rulers. God's people were forced to wonder if the city in which they dwelt would serve as a place of refuge and worship. Furthermore, the exile had made Israel into a templeless, or presenceless, people. Once back in Jerusalem, they rebuilt the temple, but a level of uncertainty remained as to whether God would dwell in their midst, if his glory would return to the temple (Ezekiel 10). The cultural mandate and the call to function as salt and light had been republished during the Babylonian exile, but history bears out that Israel became increasingly secularized, even to the point that the sacrificial system was corrupted during the period between the two testaments.

It seemed that with the exile and Israel's subsequent failure to fulfill its missional urban calling, the future of cities itself was in question. How will God approach cities now that it is clear that his people are unable to bring about the kind of renewal that he desires? Are cities to be abandoned as polarizing, irredeemable, unlivable, idolatrous places? Along with those who returned to Jerusalem from exile we wonder, "Is there a way that the city could once again be made a place of refuge?" More than that, is there a way that humanity can once again dwell in the presence of God, or will God ever again make his home in a city? Finally, are the foreshadowings of human flourishing, cultural development, and *shalom* simply to be left behind as relics of a former naive, optimistic dream? These questions hang in the air between the two testaments, and in a way we find that they make their way into our own minds. As we move into the New Testament, we find that God has a surprisingly upside-down way of answering these questions: with an unflagging, counterintuitive, self-emptying fidelity to the city.

THE CITY IN THE GOSPELS

When God's people's commitment to the urban mandate fizzled out, he personally took up responsibility for the mission, took on human flesh, and was born into the city (Luke 2:11). The significance of the incarnation of Jesus Christ is impossible to overstate. God became man to rescue his people. When we had turned the garden city into a sin-city, God broke into our history to establish, in the most upside-down manner, the foundations of a new city, untainted by sin and its effects. The Gospels are one of the primary places in Scripture where God's commitment to the city unfolds.

Jesus's Relation to the City

But what does Jesus have to do with the city? Interestingly, discussion about the person of Jesus is often where debates over the primacy of urban-versus-rural ministry come into clearest focus. It is not uncommon to hear discussions contrasting a rural Jesus to an urban Paul. But is there any substance to the view that Jesus is primarily a rural figure? Or would we be pushing it to claim that Jesus was on some sort of a mission toward a city, namely Jerusalem? Drawing on the work of Andrew Overman, Harvie Conn helpfully sets the context for this discussion by looking at the undeniably urbanized environment in which Jesus ministered:

> "One could not live in any village in lower Galilee and escape the effects and ramifications of urbanization." Life here was urbanized and urbane as anywhere else in the Empire. Did these urban influences escape the attention of Jesus and his disciples whose principal ministry was in this region? Not if we judge by a vocabulary studded with references to urban institutions like courts (Mt. 5:25) and city market squares (Mt. 23:7; Mk. 5:56), and with financial analogies built on interest-bearing accounts (Mt. 25:27; Lk. 19:23) and metaphors of God as an absentee landlord (Mk. 12:1–12). Centurion leaders of one thousand soldiers (Mt. 8:5) and bureaucratic tax collectors controlling even fishing rights (Mt. 9:10; Lk. 5:27) dot the Galilean narratives.[23]

Jesus's ministry is not only set in an urban context, we must remember that in some sense its goal—that by which it is gravitationally pulled—is a city. This is eminently clear in Luke's Gospel where the bulk of the story is shaped around Jesus's journey toward Jerusalem. The major turn of the book occurs in 9:51, where we see Jesus "[setting] his face to go to Jerusalem." The travelogue continues until Jesus enters the temple in 19:45, effectively taking Jesus to the center of the city immediately outside of which he will soon be put to death. Though it will not be a refuge for him, Jesus is determined to get to Jerusalem. To recognize the centrality of the city of Jerusalem for Jesus's ministry is not to deny or undervalue his ministry in rural and presuburban settings, it is simply to acknowledge the shape of his ministry as it is presented in Scripture. As we will see, in Jesus, God's commitment to the city is at its peak.

Jesus's Incarnation: A New Temple

Our brief survey of the Old Testament showed that God's original intention for the city was that it might be a place where he dwelt with his people. We saw this in the garden, and again clearly with the temple in Jerusalem. You'll recall that Israel's exile was essentially their being cast out of the presence of God in Jerusalem. The looming question remains: "Will God ever dwell in a city with his people again?" The radical nature of Jesus's incarnation is that it is a direct answer to this question. In Jesus, God enters into an earthly city to dwell with his people once again. And, amazingly, he does it through a new temple. But even more shockingly, the new temple is a person: Jesus.[24] All that the temple was, the new temple is . . . and more.

Jesus enters into the city of Jerusalem intent on setting himself up as the new temple (John 2:18–22). As such, he himself will be the center of a new city. During his earthly ministry he is ushering in a new community, a city on a hill (Matt. 5:14), which presently mirrors that future city with the Lamb at its center (Rev. 21:22). In this way God's condescension into this world is the entrance of an urban renewal plan, a rewriting of the history of the earthly city. Humanity and its idols will no longer be at the center of the city, rather, the renewed city will be a community gathered around Jesus.

In Christ, God is about resolving the primary question that the history of humanity and Israel have led us to ask. How can a people who were once at home in God's presence, then thrown out as a result of their sin, get back home? The answer? By fulfilling in himself the Old Testament prophecies of a day when God would once again dwell among his people, the new temple condescends to earth (John 1:14; 2:19–22; 4:20–24; 7:38–39) to become the means by which "heaven comes down to the cities of the world" and by which "we ascend to the heavenly city."[25] Jesus came to the earthly city to make a way for us to enter the heavenly city (Hebrews 11)!

Jesus's Experience of the Brokenness of the City

That God came to dwell among men is earth-shattering in itself. That he would willingly identify with us to the point of experiencing all of our pain, temptation, and sorrow takes the story of redemption to a new level (Heb. 4:15). As Jesus moves toward Jerusalem, he experiences the full brokenness of the earthly city. Jesus comes into contact with and is ultimately the victim of all that is wrong with cities marked by sin. Though it is his city, "the city of the great King" (Matt. 5:35), the Gospels present a picture of Jerusalem turning on Jesus.

In some sense it is no surprise to find Jerusalem full of upwardly mobile professionals who are maximizing their potential for idolatrous self-gain—that is something we find in our own fallen cities. Jesus regularly interacts with corrupt religious professionals seeking to maintain their position and comfort, even if the cost is eliminating him from the picture (Mark 3:6). The trial that leads to his death is overseen by legal professionals more concerned with their acceptance by the crowds than rightly carrying out justice (John 19:1–16). Even the soldiers who oversee his death greedily gamble for a dying man's robe (Matt. 27:35). It is clear that Jesus suffers at the hands of a city that has been utterly swayed by the idols of the human heart. Jerusalem has become the unfaithful, whoring city of Isaiah 1. How will it once again be called just and righteous? How will a city that Jesus calls "forsaken" (Luke 13:35) ever again be called "Sought Out, A City Not Forsaken" (Isa. 62:12)?

Jesus's Death and Resurrection in Light of the City

Immediately before he enters center-city Jerusalem, Jesus stops to look at and ponder the city. There is something about city skylines and densely populated spaces that inspire awe and excitement in us, but when Jesus looked at his city, he was driven to weeping (Luke 19:41). Jesus weeps three times in Scripture: over the death of Lazarus (John 11:35), over his own impending death (Heb. 5:7), and here over the death of judgment that was to befall Jerusalem. Essentially, Jesus is mourning the death of his city.

What's most remarkable is Jesus's action following this episode of city mourning. He could have turned his back on the city, leaving it to be destroyed. Or, perhaps, he could have judged it himself at that moment. Instead, what we find is Jesus charging headlong into the center of the city and taking up a daily teaching post at the temple despite intense opposition from the religious authorities (Luke 19:45–48). There, tensions rise: the people are continually captivated by Jesus, while the religious leaders' intentions grow increasingly violent.

As we track with the authors of the Gospels, we find that Jesus's entrance into Jerusalem is more than just a haphazard change of location. If the scriptural claim that Jesus is God incarnate is true, then in this narrative we have the momentous entrance of the presence of God into a city to dwell with his people. God once again dwells in the city as he did at the establishment of the first temple. The shock is that those who appear most eager to preserve, maintain, and honor traditions based upon the presence of God in the temple want nothing to do with God when he personally arrives in their city. In this way, Jerusalem essentially becomes the ultimate expression of the rebellious city of man. Even when God forces his way into their midst, they refuse to let him reign, but insist on ruling their city, their lives, and even their religion without reference to his presence. Jerusalem, the city of the great King, displays the very height of human sin and depravity when the city votes by mob rule to execute its great King.

How can an unfaithful, forsaken city become "Not Forsaken" (Isa. 62:12)? The answer lies in the upside-down wisdom of the cross. In the crucifixion of Jesus Christ, God takes the antagonism, hostility, and violence of the inhabitants of the earthly city upon himself. Jesus, God's Son, is forsaken (Matt. 27:46) in order that he might create a city called "Not Forsaken." He faithfully bears the punishment for our unfaithfulness so that his city can be called righteous and faithful (Isa. 1:26). Ironically, the intensified evil of the city of man is the very instrument that God providentially uses to bring about the city's salvation: Jesus's death will ultimately win life for a city of people who have rejected him.

To put the question another way: how can a presenceless people be welcomed into God's presence once again? The events that surround Jesus's death show a bit more of what is actually happening at the cross. The Synoptic Gospels all tell us that during Jesus's crucifixion the curtain of the temple was torn in two from top to bottom (Matt. 27:51; Mark 15:38; Luke 23:45). The symbolic meaning of this tearing is that in order for open access to the presence of God to be given to his people, judgment had to fall. And, if judgment was not going to be placed upon the people, it had to be placed upon God himself. In light of the fact that the New Testament authors understand Jesus to be the new temple, his crucifixion can be understood in part as the judgment of God falling upon the new temple. As Jesus is figuratively torn in two at the cross, open access to God's presence is now given to those who approach God through Christ.[26] At the cross, global access to his presence is granted through the tearing of the curtain of the new temple, namely Jesus!

When Jesus made the claim that he himself was the new temple, he had predicted his death. However, he also predicted his resurrection, claiming that he would rise again after three days (John 2:19). In this radical event in redemptive history, Jesus overcame death and became the firstfruits of a new creation (1 Cor. 15:20; Rom. 8:23). In the resurrection we glimpse the fulfillment of the promise of the new heavens and a new earth, the center of which will be a bustling city.

Summary

The Gospels show us that in his birth, life, death, and resurrection, Jesus was concerned to enter fully into our earthly cities, to be present as God in the city of the great King, to turn a forsaken, presenceless people into a "not forsaken," presence-blessed people, and to establish the foundations of a future new creational city in which he and his people will dwell together forever. In essence, Jesus gave up the comforts, power, and control of the city that was, to gain that city that will be, toward which we work for the *shalom* of the city that now is.[27] The matter of what happens in cities between Jesus's first and second coming is taken up with the Acts of the Apostles.

ACTS

Luke, a companion of the apostles, and one concerned with communicating the truth about Jesus, wrote not only a Gospel, but also a book detailing the beginning and expansion of the early church. In light of the fact that Luke's Gospel was ordered around Jesus's journey *to* Jerusalem, it is not surprising but certainly important that Acts begins in and is structured around the way that the gospel moves out *from* Jerusalem. And, just as *a* city was the geographical focus of his Gospel narrative, *cities* will be the geographical focus of Acts.[28]

The earliest chapters of Acts find an infant church that is radically generous, organically communal, intentionally devotional, boldly evangelistic, and distinctly urban (Acts 2:42–47; 1:4). Most readers would happily agree with the first four descriptors, but it may be that some find themselves uncomfortable with the last. Was the earliest church really "distinctly urban"? The answer must be yes, if only because Jesus himself confined the early church to Jerusalem as they waited for the infilling of the Holy Spirit (1:4). The resulting question is, "As it grew, did the early church remain distinctly urban?"[29]

God's original Edenic intention for the geographic expansion of the place of his presence is seen working itself out in the life of the church.[30] Interestingly, it is persecution that we find scattering the church "throughout the regions of Judea and Samaria" (8:1). The keen reader will recall that in 1:8, Jesus had outlined their missional calling as one that would move them from Jerusalem to Judea, Samaria, and, ultimately, "the end of the earth," namely to Rome and beyond. In essence, it is through this persecution that the church is launched out on mission. By Acts 11, Christians who were scattered had traveled to port cities and important islands in the Mediterranean where the gospel naturally began to spread to the Gentiles. At each step we see scattered Christians migrating to important cities and influential regions. With the beginning of chapter 13 there is a shift of geographical focus from one city (Jerusalem) to another (Antioch), from a largely Jewish city to a radically diverse metropolis. The religious center and the capital of Christianity has shifted from one major city to another major city. It has moved from its Jerusalem-based, Judaism-oriented origins, and is now an increasingly Gentile movement based in a Gentile city. This city will act as the starting point for all three of the apostle Paul's missionary journeys (chaps. 13, 15, 18).

As we track with Luke through Acts, it is clear that Jesus Christ has created a church that is bent toward geographical expansion that happens primarily in cities.

> The world that we enter in the book of Acts is the most modern in all the Bible by virtue of its urban identity. Most of the action occurs in the famous cities of the Greco-Roman world, not in the local villages or the countryside. This prevailingly metropolitan world is, moreover, international and cosmopolitan. There is a sense in which the city is vindicated in the history of the early church—not in the sense that the city is mainly good or cordial to the gospel but in the sense that the city is where most people now live and where the influential power structures exist. . . . *It is easy to see that the mission strategy of the early church was to evangelize the city.* It is no exaggeration to say that in Acts the church is almost exclusively associated with the city.[31]

While we must be careful to read Acts descriptively rather than prescriptively, it is hard to ignore the strategic nature of the spread of the gospel in and through cities. "It seems to have been Paul's deliberate policy to move purposefully from one strategic city-centre to the next."[32] This is perhaps most notable and noticeable in the ministry of Paul. Take for example his ministry locales in Acts 17–19. In chapter 17 alone we find him in Thessalonica (the primary trade city in Macedonia), Berea (a central artistic and agricultural city), and at the Areopagus in Athens (a key city for thought, discussion, and religion in the Hellenistic world). Chapter 18 puts Paul in the middle of the hub of economic prosperity and pagan immorality: Corinth. And in chapter 19 we follow Paul to Ephesus—a large city where religion, trade, and artisanship combined to create one of the most influential urban centers of the New Testament era.

Are we being selective here, simply highlighting the ministry that occurred in big cities? If so, it is because the author of Luke maintains the same selectivity. As Conn notes, "It is no exaggeration to say that the book of Acts deals almost entirely with cities; missionary work is almost limited to them."[33] Even Adolf von Harnack, a liberal scholar with no interest in mission, let alone urban ministry, sees this same pattern in Acts: "The mission was for the most part carried out in cities, as also the Jews of the Diaspora were chiefly settled in cities." Von Harnack goes on to note that city locales are so assumed in Luke that the author must point out when something takes place outside the city (7:58; 14:19; 16:13; 21:5).[34]

With Acts moving toward its conclusion, Luke begins to shape his final chapters around Paul's journey toward Rome, the capital of the Empire. In short, were Paul to reach Rome, Jesus's commission of his witnesses "to the end of the earth" would reach its initial stage of fulfillment. Of all the cities Paul saw, of all the churches he planted, he is set on personally bringing the gospel to the most influential city in the world. Facing personal opposition, imprisonment, shipwreck, and more, Paul did not quit until he arrived in Rome. And once in Rome, Paul stayed in the city: his mission had reached its goal. Tradition tells us that Paul remained in the capital city until his martyrdom, reminding us that the gospel will not always be welcome in influential places.

The world of Acts was cosmopolitan, pluralistic, and distinctly urban. The early church, though certainly not ignoring the villages and countryside, placed a strategic priority on bringing the gospel to and establishing new churches in cities.[35] Through the power of the Holy Spirit, the gospel of Jesus Christ created a radical community that expanded geographically throughout an entire empire. The similarities to our own day are too glaring to overlook. As we view our increasingly urban world that is serving to create a widespread cosmopolitan, pluralistic spirit, could it be that we stand on the edge of a new movement of the gospel in the cities of our world? With millions flocking to cities, seeing them as centers of innovation, refuge, comfort, and more, could it be the case that the gospel will be what ultimately captures their imaginations? Will cities continue to be the locations through which the church brings the gospel "to the end of the earth"?

PAULINE EPISTLES

Having seen the strategic urban focus of the mission of the church in the book of Acts, when we arrive in the Epistles it is only natural to wonder why there are so few references to the city in Paul's letters. If to this point the New Testament has been moving toward a city, and the message of the gospel has been moving out into cities, why do we hear so little about the city in the apostolic letters? Paul himself only uses the Greek word for city (*polis*) four times in his writings, and each of those occurrences is somewhat circumstantial, certainly never central to his argument. Is there a disconnect here? Has a shift away from cities taken place?

The answer to these questions lies in the same circumstantial, infrequent use of city terminology in Paul's epistles that one might use to argue against reading Paul as distinctly urban.[36] Contrary to first appearances, his epistolary writings are even more urban than we think. Without exception, his letters are written from cities to cities. His ministry to these respective urban churches is a reflection or description of the geographic expansion of urban church planting.

This being the case, we are able to see why he uses little explicit city terminology. He does not need to argue for the necessity of ministry in cities; he can assume it. He does not need to argue for a recovery of emphasis on urban mission because he and his fellow Christians are living it out. The city, the *polis*, was the very air that Paul and his urban readers were breathing. Paul's ministry happened in cities.

Normally, we might quickly look over a verse like Romans 16:23, which sends greetings to the church at Rome from "Erastus, the city treasurer." But this is exactly the kind of evidence a historian would be looking for to determine where Paul did his ministry, as well as the types of persons it was impacting. This is an indication that through Paul's ministry, the gospel had made its way even into the heart of the treasurer of the city of Corinth, which was a significant engine of economic production. On top of this, Erastus had settled himself into the Corinthian community and understood himself to be connected to the Christians in the city of Rome.

In sum, Paul was an urban dweller whose life, ministry, writing, and death took place in cities. "Paul was a city person. The city breathes through his language."[37] The result of his ministry was a network of vibrant city churches full of city Christians. Though he nowhere develops a theology of the city in his letters, his life is a veritable practical theology in the city. Paul's life and writings are the hands-on application of what is seen to be happening in cities throughout the book of Acts.

HEBREWS

What we've said about the absence of explicit references to the city in Paul can equally be applied to the General Epistles, with one glaring exception. Apart from Revelation, there is no other New Testament book that addresses the topic of a theology of the city more clearly than the book of Hebrews. Three passages in particular, found in the latter half of the book, provide nuance and clarity to a biblical theology of the city.

Looking Toward a Future City

In Hebrews 11, where we read about many of the heroes of the faith, the author of the epistle leads us to consider Abraham. Called by God to leave his birth city, Abraham was one who lived "in tents" on the way to the land of promise (v. 9). The author's assumption is that this was not an ideal way of life; Abraham would have desired to settle down in a city. However, by faith, Abraham chose to believe in God's promise of a future land inheritance. In this way, Hebrews says that he was "looking forward to the city that has foundations, whose designer and builder is God" (v. 10). The text goes on to say that Abraham and his family could have returned to their homeland, but set their faces toward "a better country." And what destination were they anticipating? "God . . . has prepared for them a city" (v. 16).

There is a future city, and its builder is God. At least one of the ways that we relate to that future city is to look forward to it with eager anticipation. This is the "not-yet" aspect of the future city of God. Along with the heroes of the faith in Hebrews 11, we are all en route to a new God-designed city. We are sojourners and exiles seeking a homecoming to the garden city of God. A clear understanding of this will keep us from ever simply equating our earthly cities with that city which is to come. Yet it also assures us that God is a lover of cities; he is the ultimate city planner. When he seeks to build a place that will fulfill all of his covenant promises to Abraham, he builds a city.

Experiencing a Future City Now

Hebrews 12 finds the author seeking to encourage his audience of tempted believers. He is speaking to a scattered group of Jewish Christians who find the idea of reverting back to Judaism alluring. Tempted by the comforts of the system and traditions out of which they were saved, these Christians have begun to doubt that Christ can provide for them what they had experienced in their past religious lives. The writer's response is to stack up in marvelous style a list of the unseeable, unsearchable, unfathomable access and blessings that they have in Christ. In contrast to the Israelites who were made to tremble at the presence of God, unable even to approach Mount Sinai, Christians are said to "have come to Mount Zion and to the city of the living God, the heavenly Jerusalem" (12:22). The author essentially tells them, "You need to know that you are now experiencing, in an already/not-yet manner, that city toward which your forefathers looked."

So, whereas chapter 11 spoke of the God-built city as something that we might look forward to but not yet experience in full, chapter 12 speaks of "the city of the living God, the heavenly Jerusalem," as something that we have "come to" already (v. 22).[38] No one would deny that the Christian has presently "come to" Jesus, has been sprinkled with his blood, and has been made part of the communion of saints. In the same way, we should also recognize that the Christian has been made a present participant in "the city of the living God." The expected future "city of God has invaded invisibly into the present age in order that saints may now be able to participate in it."[39] The net result of this already/not-yet experience of God's future city is that we are presently living as citizens of two cities: the earthly city and the heavenly city. The latter citizenship, which forms our primary identity, informs the way we live, work, and play in the former. But on what basis is such an already/not-yet participation and citizenship offered to believers?

Establishment of the Future City

As we surveyed the Old Testament material on the city, one of the primary motifs that emerged was that of refuge. Known for fortified walls and well-functioning legal systems, cities were the place for marginalized, poor, and even fugitive people to find safety. When Israel was exiled from the presence of God, they lost not only access to the temple, but also the safety of the city of the great King. The removal of sin from the city was the only way that Israel could remain in the refuge-presence of God (Ex. 29:14), and when the sacrificial system was ultimately unable to remove the sin of the people, the people themselves had to be removed from the safety of God's presence. How, then, can God's people hope to be restored to the refuge of the city of the great King?

Hebrews 13 shows us the way. There we are told that in his crucifixion, "Jesus . . . suffered outside the gate in order to sanctify the people through his own blood" (v. 12). At the cross Jesus forgoes the refuge of the earthly city, is expelled from God's presence, and perfectly bears the sins of the people. The result is the establishment of a future city, "the city that is to come," in which God's people will forever enjoy the refuge and comfort of his presence, uninhibited by sin (v. 14). This has immense significance for the way we presently live our lives. Because through faith we live in communion with God and mysteriously experience the refuge of that future city, we are now able to have a realistic perspective on and relationship to our cities. Even as we live deeply connected lives in our present cities, we understand ourselves to be dual citizens who do not ultimately derive acceptance, approval, comfort, and refuge from them (v. 13). To paraphrase Keller, we are citizens of one city, yet full-time residents of another. Our primary allegiance is given to a city from which we derive our most formative beliefs and practices. And yet we live in our cities of residence as full participants. We do not live as natives, tourists, or travelers; we are "resident aliens."[40] Because in Christ we now experience in an already/not-yet manner the benefits of perfect relationship with God in that future city, we can rightly interpret the blessings of the earthly city as a promissory down payment of that city that is to come.[41] "By his grace, Jesus lost the city-that-was, so we could become citizens of the city-to-come, making us salt and light in the city-that-is."[42]

REVELATION

If the narrative of the Old Testament left us wondering how God could dwell in the city again with his people, and if Jesus's death and resurrection established a way for that to happen, then the book of Revelation gives us a glimpse into that beautiful future. The book itself is addressed to seven city churches in Asia (1:4; 2–3), and it serves to challenge and encourage them in their faith by revealing the final triumph of Christ. That triumph leads to the consummation of the centerpiece of the new creation, which is an indescribable city.

Though the book is written to specific first-century churches, its writer looks forward to a time when the geographical expansion of God's kingdom will have reached the end of the earth. Christians "from every nation, from all tribes and peoples and languages" will one day gather around Jesus to worship him for the salvation he has won (7:9–10). The Christian community believed that in order to reach all tribes, peoples, and languages, it needed to reach the cities of the world.

But Revelation is far more than a roll call of nations; it is a future vision of the final triumph of God over his enemies, and the consummation of a new creation. Interestingly, the cosmic battle that leads to an eternally peaceful new world is cast in the language of cities. All that is wrong with this present world as a result of human sin is symbolized in Revelation as "Babylon." As final judgment is declared upon this enemy of God and his people, onlookers cry out, "Alas! Alas! You great city, you mighty city, Babylon! For in a single hour your judgment has come" (18:10). Following this judgment, there is great rejoicing in heaven because God's redemptive plan to bring a people into eternal communion with himself is coming to completion. The sinful, fallen, earthly city has been judged, making way for a new city.

As Babylon smolders, a group of sailors looks on and asks, "What city was like the great city?" (18:18). The question is a natural one and leads to others. Will Babylon rise again? Do cities simply disappear with God's righteous judgment? Were cities just the result of the fall, and are they simply eliminated when God sets things right? Revelation's answer to these questions is a resounding *no*. In eliminating the city of Babylon, God put on display his ultimate commitment to *his* city. Nothing more would stand in the way between him and a perfect relationship to his people in a densely populated, racially mixed, metropolitan human settlement.

In Revelation 21 we see the consummation of a new heaven and a new earth (vv. 1–8), and at the center of the new earth is that future city to which we have been referring in these pages. The passage is worth quoting at length as it is remarkable in what it describes and impossible to top:

> And he carried me away in the Spirit to a great, high mountain, and showed me the holy city Jerusalem coming down out of heaven from God, having the glory of God, its radiance like a most rare jewel, like a jasper, clear as crystal. It had a great, high wall, with twelve gates, and at the gates twelve angels, and on the gates the names of the twelve tribes of the sons of Israel were inscribed—on the east three gates, on the north three gates, on the south three gates, and on the west three gates. And the wall of the city had twelve foundations, and on them were the twelve names of the twelve apostles of the Lamb.
>
> And the one who spoke with me had a measuring rod of gold to measure the city and its gates and walls. The city lies foursquare, its length the same as its width. And he measured the city with his rod, 12,000 stadia. Its length and width and height are equal. He also measured its wall, 144 cubits by human measurement, which is also an angel's measurement. The wall was built of jasper, while the city was pure gold, like clear glass. The foundations of the wall of the city were adorned with every kind of jewel. The first was jasper, the second sapphire, the third agate, the fourth emerald, the fifth onyx, the sixth carnelian, the seventh chrysolite, the eighth beryl, the ninth topaz, the tenth chrysoprase, the eleventh jacinth, the twelfth amethyst. And the twelve gates were twelve pearls, each of the gates made of a single pearl, and the street of the city was pure gold, like transparent glass.
>
> And I saw no temple in the city, for its temple is the Lord God the Almighty and the Lamb. And the city has no need of sun or moon to shine on it, for the glory of God gives it light, and its lamp is the Lamb. By its light will the nations walk, and the kings of the earth will bring their glory into it, and its gates will never be shut by day—and there will be no night there. They will bring into it the glory and the honor of the nations. But nothing unclean will ever enter it, nor

anyone who does what is detestable or false, but only those who are written in the Lamb's book of life. (Rev. 21:10–27)

An entire book could be devoted to these verses. There is much to say in terms of measurements and numbers, jewels and allusions to Old Testament prophecy. But we'll focus on just a few items.

First, note that the city is very material and cultural. It features things like walls, gates, streets, inscriptions, and fine jewels. In other words, the future city is a cultural masterpiece. Second, the enormous, God-built walls show us that our future urban home is a perfect place of refuge. Third, the city has gates, but they are always open. There is never fear of invasion or intrusion; nothing will ever enter the city that is displeasing or opposed to God. Finally, and most astoundingly, there is no temple in the city. Because all of the city's inhabitants have been cleansed by the blood of Christ, they are able to live in a perfect, unmediated, no-temple relationship with God. In short, all that the city was ever meant to be, but failed to be, one day it *will be* in the New Jerusalem. All of the following are promised in the new city: cultural diversity and development, refuge and comfort, human flourishing and harmonious fellowship, creativity and connective diversity, and unhindered proximity to the presence of God in the context of constant worship. The city of Revelation 21 is essentially our return to the garden of Eden in an escalated, more glorious fashion. And that new city is our future home.

CONCLUSION

When we consider the sweep of redemptive history, we see the ultimate wisdom of God in Christ, and his unwillingness to abandon his desire to dwell with his people in a city. Beginning with Adam and Eve, we saw a picture of individuals living in a flourishing garden city that afforded unhindered access to God's presence. As a result of the exile of the fall, they were cast out of God's presence. We were left to wonder, "How do we get back into the garden city?"

With Israel, God chose a people to be his own. He set them up in the city of Jerusalem and promised to dwell in their midst by way of the temple. Their continual disobedience led to exile from the city and God's presence. We were left to wonder, "How do we get back to a city in which the presence of God dwells?"

God's answer to these questions is found in the person and work of Jesus Christ. Though he was located securely in heaven, fully enjoying the benefits of an unhindered relationship within the life of the Trinity, Jesus willingly gave up the comforts of heaven and condescended to earth in his incarnation. Having lived the perfect life that both Adam and Israel failed to live, Jesus went on willingly to suffer the exile and forsakenness of the cross. By fulfilling the original calling of both Adam and Israel, and substitutionarily bearing the punishment that sinners deserve, Jesus rewrites history and opens up a way for us to return to a right relationship with God. This is how we get back into the presence of God, into a city where God dwells!

In Christ, we who were separated from God by the slavery and exile of sin are now given free access to his presence by way of the new temple, Jesus Christ. And amazingly, it is on the foundation of his death and resurrection that we are given citizenship and a future permanent residence in a new city. In that city we will enjoy unhindered relationship with God and one another for all eternity. Ruled by the great King, that city will be *the* center of power. Populated by a flourishing, new-creational, redeemed humanity, that city will be *the* center of culture. Filled with the presence of God and a dense, diverse population of former idolaters who have been set free, that city will be *the* center of worship.

From start to finish, the Bible presents to us a God who is committed to providing a city in which he can dwell with his people. The extent to which he goes to build that city is shocking. The promise of that perfect, future city has, in an already/not-yet fashion, broken into our present lives. Having been captured by the gospel and made citizens of the heavenly city, we are now uniquely equipped to live, work, and play as salt and light in our respective earthly cities. The chapters that follow will encourage you to think deeply about what it will look like for you to live missionally in your city, in light of God's (literal) dying and undying commitment to it.

DISCUSSION QUESTIONS

1. Prior to having read this chapter, what were your thoughts about the Bible's perspective on the city? How has your perspective changed? Do you agree with the authors that cities are God's invention and at least a part of his intention for the world?

2. What do you think about this statement from Meredith Kline: "The ultimate goal set before humanity at the very beginning was that human culture should take city-form"? What about the garden of Eden hints at God's plans for cultural cultivation and development?

3. How do you interpret Jeremiah 29:7 "But seek the welfare of the city where I have sent you into exile, and pray to the LORD on its behalf, for in its welfare you will find your welfare"? What are the implications for Christians today? What would it look like for you to seek the welfare of the city in which God has placed you?

4. What do you make of the book of Acts' strategic focus on cities? How can it be said that "the mission strategy of the early church was to evangelize the city"? If this is true, how should it shape our understanding and practice of evangelization? Is there a way for the church to respond to rapid global urbanization while ensuring that we do not neglect the equally important rural and suburban mission fields?

5. Why do you think that God's plan of redemption culminates in a city where he dwells with his people? In what ways will that city look like the cities of our own day? In what ways will it look different?

Chapter 4

CONTEXTUALIZATION IN THE CITY

No truth which human beings may articulate can ever be articulated in a culture-transcending way—but that does not mean that the truth thus articulated does not transcend culture.[1]

D. A. Carson

Every thoughtful Christian wants to know how to practically live out their Christian life in a secular culture. This concern has only become more pressing in our increasingly post-Christian world.[2] We wonder, "How can I engage my culture in a meaningful, winsome way without compromising my biblical convictions, but at the same time live in a way that is not abrasive and religious?" "How can I live as a Christian in a secular city like Boston or San Francisco without becoming Boston-ized or San Francisco-ized?" Since San Francisco and heaven represent two very different cultures, we tend to think that we must choose one over the other—either be a San Franciscan or a Christian. This is a mistake. Abandoning our worldview or privatizing our worldview are not the only options.

As we saw in Jeremiah 28–29 with the exilic experience of Daniel and the other Israelite professionals, the Bible does not limit us to choose between compromise or retreat in relating to our pluralistic world. The God of the Bible commissions Christians to be spiritually bicultural. Christians are summoned to enter into the city of man while remaining citizens of the city of God.[3] The Scriptures obviously do not tell us to love the city and hate God, nor does God ask us to love him and hate the city—the call is to love both God and the city. What does this look like? How can the church deeply engage the city and at the same time live as a distinctive society?

SEEKING THE WELFARE OF THE CITY

As Jeremiah 29:7 commands, we are to pray for the city and seek its welfare. We're told that in seeking the *shalom* of the city, we will find our welfare. In other words, if the city prospers, then you will prosper also. This Hebrew word *shalom* (translated here as "welfare") means complete well-being, universal flourishing, wholeness, delight, and blessing. It is "a rich state of affairs in which natural needs are satisfied and natural gifts fruitfully employed, a state of affairs that inspires joyful wonder as its Creator and Savior opens doors and welcomes the creatures in whom he delights."[4] It is a description of multidimensional wholeness and flourishing that is not just spiritual, but also material, physical, psychological, and economic.

This *shalom* will not come through Christians establishing parallel subcultural institutions, but through a conviction to bring comprehensive renewal to the city by pursuing its common good.[5] Many urban folks that we know often think thoughts like: "I know I'm supposed to be here because our church always emphasizes that we're city positive, but I'm getting worn out. There's so much pollution and noise and stress in the city that I'd like to move to the mountains of New Hampshire or Lake Tahoe. It's so quiet and beautiful there, maybe I'd be more happy there." By default, we assume that being outside the city is good and living inside the city is bad. Indeed, "most Christians read the Bible through rural lenses."[6] But the city is where culture is shaped. The city is where the people live.[7] And God loves people! And since cities are full of people, we know that God really loves cities. As Tim Keller states, "Because the world is on its way to becoming 70 percent urban, we all need a theological vision that is distinctly urban. Even if you don't go to the city to minister, make no mistake: the city is coming to you."[8]

Why do cities matter? Cities matter because people matter.

At the risk of overstatement, Bill Crispin argues that cities matter because there is a high concentration of people: "The city is the place where there are more people . . . [and since] God loves people . . . [we can be assured that] He loves the city."[9]

Culture is established in cities—the places where diverse people are most densely congregated together to live, work, worship, create, learn, and play. Scripture calls us to align our lives and talents with the missional heart of God by contributing to our culture's common good—by making a serious contribution to our city's art, business, music, law, literature, education, medicine, finance, etc. We see a perfect picture of this in Jesus Christ who came to earth in the ultimate contextualized way. Jesus did not undercontextualize his incarnation—he did not commute to Jerusalem from heaven—but through his incarnation, Jesus left heaven and took up residence in an earthly city and engaged a fallen humanity in order to redeem it.

A CITY SHAPED BY KINGDOM VALUES

All people, institutions, and groups are interested in changing and transforming society by impressing their core values on the culture. None of us has a choice in making an impact on our culture. The minute anyone opens his mouth, he is speaking in a particular language, from a particular cultural context, with a particular worldview of morality and various definitions of what he believes to be true, good, and beautiful. No one should be led to think that he is not getting into the public square. You cannot *not* impact your city and culture.

The question is, "In what particular way are you impacting your city and culture?" Engagement isn't optional. What is optional is the type of impact one makes.

In addressing the question, "Is it the church's responsibility to embrace the civic responsibility of the city (e.g., education, the poor, social injustice, the arts, etc.)?" we need to consider the following. The institutional church does not have juridical authority in the city/state public square, but that does not mean that the organic church ought to stay outside on the periphery.[10] Christians have the responsibility to act in mercy and to engage our community with deeds of social justice. Paul states in Galatians 6:10, "As we have opportunity, let us do good to all people, especially to those who belong to the family of believers" (NIV). James says that true religion is this: "To look after orphans and widows in their distress and to keep oneself from being polluted by the world" (1:27 NIV). In other words, it is the church's responsibility to pursue both public compassion and personal piety. For example, although a failing public school system is not the civic responsibility of the church, the church may well get involved in "doing good" by coming alongside the local school in providing after-school tutoring or other assistance.

Christians ought to cultivate friendships with people in their neighborhoods and cities. This may well mean joining clubs and associations, and partnering with organizations that are also involved in acts of mercy and benevolence. None of this means that the primacy of proclaiming the gospel is undermined. Rather, as the gospel is proclaimed in our churches and in our cities, the effect of this gospel preaching, the entailment of the gospel,[11] will be the transformation of men and women such that we begin to love our neighbors where once we loved only ourselves.

> This pattern so contradicts the thinking and practice of the world, that it creates an "alternate kingdom," an "alternate city" (Matt. 5:14–16) in which there is a complete reversal of the values of the world with regard to power, recognition, status, wealth. The gospel reverses the place of the weak and the strong, the "outsider" and the "insider." It is an advantage, spiritually speaking, to see one's weakness; it is a severe danger, spiritually speaking, to be successful and accomplished. And when we finally understand that we can be saved by sheer grace through Christ, we stop seeking salvation (either that of psychological fulfillment, or of social transformation, or of spiritual blessing, or of all three) in power, status and accomplishment. That destroys their power in our lives. The reversal of the cross, the grace of God, thus liberates us from bondage to [the] power of material things and worldly status in our lives. We begin to live a new life without much regard to them.[12]

Some people live in the city and find their needs met there: they obtain credentials, status, education, training, and influence. Others are almost consumed by the city. But Christians approach the city differently. Christians desire to live counterculturally in the city. Christians participate in the in-breaking of God's kingdom among a people he has claimed as his own as he forms them into a distinct, set-apart community that looks forward to the full arrival of his authority and presence in the world. Christians don't come to the city to take; we come to the city to give.

ABANDONING YOUR WORLDVIEW IN THE CITY

Christians tend to make two very different but equally damaging mistakes in their approach to the city: abandoning their worldview or privatizing their worldview. Neither of these outcomes happens overnight—these are trajectories that begin as one first takes on a posture toward the city. Both individuals and churches can make these mistakes which, to put in other words, are issues of overcontextualization or undercontextualization:[13]

> To reach people we must appreciate and adapt to their culture, but we must also challenge and confront it. This is based on the biblical teaching that all cultures have God's grace and natural revelation in them, yet they are also in rebellious idolatry. If we overadapt to a culture, we have accepted the culture's idols. If, however, we underadapt to a culture, we may have turned our own culture into an idol, an absolute. If we overadapt to a culture, we aren't able to change people because we are not calling them to change. If we underadapt to a culture, no one will be changed because no one will listen to us; we will be confusing, offensive, or simply unpersuasive. To the degree a ministry is overadapted or underadapted to a culture, it loses life-changing power.[14]

We've watched many well-meaning believers abandon their Christian convictions for the sake of assimilating into the life of the city. A young graduate moves to London to work for an investment firm. He arrives in hopes of "making it big" and securing a successful future for himself. He loves God and gets involved in a good church. But his driving desire to "make it" in the city, coupled with the pace, pressure, competition, and forces of greed in London eventually results in a man whose Christianity appears to have worn away. This individual, who becomes a managing partner at the firm, has spent the last five years conforming his life to the culture of his organization and his city. In the process he has left behind a once seemingly robust biblical worldview. Through his overadaptation, his Christianity has now morphed into a secular worldview.

Often what drives the abandonment of one's worldview in the city is idolatry. In the case of our young graduate, his worship of money and success—two of the great idols of London—has changed his initial posture toward the city into a near total assimilation into London's prevailing cultural story.

Every city has its unique idols. Idolatry isn't just an individual human problem, it's a city problem. Silicon Valley has success. Sydney has pleasure. Washington, DC, has power. And many Christians approach their cities as unwitting worshipers of idols—the false gods— of their city, hoping to fill their lives with the success, pleasure, or power that their city offers. When you idolize a city, when you look to it to give you something that only God can give you, namely, salvation, flourishing, joy, and influence, you will gradually find yourself abandoning your Christian commitments in the city. What happens is actually a replacement of your beliefs. You don't merely abandon your Christian worldview, you adopt your city's baseline cultural narrative, aligning your life to worship what your city worships.

We abandon our worldview in order to use the city. We use the city to achieve our goals and dreams. Ironically, when you use the city, the city ends up using you. When we approach our cities as places to be used for our own ends, worshiping what we think the city's idols can give us, eventually we discover that the city doesn't fulfill us in the ways we had hoped.

A therapist in Silicon Valley reports that there are two types of people she sees in her counseling practice. The first type of person came to Silicon Valley hoping to make it, but he didn't make it, so he is unsatisfied. The second individual came hoping to make it, and he *did* make it, but he is also unsatisfied. If you abandon your worldview to accommodate and achieve your dreams in your city, whether you fail or succeed at your goals, you'll be left unfulfilled. Our cities are not meant to carry the weight of our worship.

PRIVATIZING YOUR WORLDVIEW IN THE CITY

The idols of a city often lead Christians to abandon their faith. However, almost as often, they lead Christians to privatize their faith. Abandonment and privatization both happen over time, but the latter is particularly subtle. In fact, urban Christians may be prone to privatize their commitment to the gospel without even knowing it.

We are all familiar with the idea that Christians are to be "in the world but not of it." This concept is derived from John 17 where Jesus acknowledges that his disciples are "*in* the world" (v. 11), while also stating that "they are *not of* the world" (v. 16). His prayer to the Father does not ease the tension, but upholds it: "I do not ask that you take them out of the world, but that you keep them from the evil one" (v. 15). Christians have wrestled with this tension since the church's beginnings, often stressing one end of the spectrum over the other. Easing the tension by drifting in either direction—by emphasizing either being *in* the world or *not of* it—will lead to faith privatization.

Those with an overconcern for being *in* the world will tend toward silence in matters of faith. The gospel will be viewed as something that is personal and individualistic. A soloist in a leading ballet company may avoid any and all reference to her faith because of the change it would make in how she is perceived by her artistic director. She may even have good intentions—she's being a "silent witness," she will share her faith once she has "made it"—but the gospel is ultimately something that she keeps to herself. Her aspirations have taken primacy over her faith, and she has made her relationship with Jesus a private matter. Her greatest fear is exclusion from the city, and she is willing to privatize her faith in order to be welcomed, accepted, and approved by her peers.

Those with an overconcern for being *not of* the world will gravitate toward separation in matters of faith. The gospel will be viewed as something that must be protected and preserved from the ruling idols of the city. A young couple lives in the city because the husband's residency at a leading hospital requires him to work long, arduous hours. The city was not their preferred living environment, and when they had their first child they went to great measures to make sure that their growing family remained safe, secure, and unstained by the darker elements of the city. Though the husband is quite vocal about his faith, his increasingly combative stance toward his coworkers and the culture at large has essentially nullified the opportunity for meaningful relationships. His separatistic approach to the city means that he and his wife do not know their neighbors and have failed to make new friends. Their self-perceived marginalization by the distasteful city culture means that, whether they like it or not, their faith has become a private matter. Their greatest fear was overidentification with the city, and they were willing to privatize the gospel to maintain safety, security, and comfort.

In both cases there is a lack of belief in the thickness of the gospel. The ballet dancer believes that her faith will cause her to be perceived as an inferior. She has chosen to find her acceptance, approval, and acclaim in her company rather than in Christ. The result is that she is silent and overly pliable. The young husband believes that his faith makes him superior. He has chosen to build walls of safety, security, and comfort, rather than trusting that God is the only one who actually provides these things for his family. The result is that he is separatistic and overly rigid. Both have forfeited a personal knowledge of the deep-reaching benefits of the gospel, and both have privatized their faith. Ultimately, when you privatize your Christian worldview, when you keep the message of Christianity to yourself and don't engage the world with it, you actually abandon the Christian worldview. The essence of Christianity is public, not private.

Common Denominator: Self-Centeredness

Abandoning the Christian worldview and privatizing the Christian worldview share a common denominator: self-centeredness. When you abandon your worldview in the city, you're choosing to look out simply for your own interests and comfort rather than work through the difficulty of living out the Christian faith in your city's unique context, with all of its challenges and opportunities. And when you privatize your Christianity you're doing the same thing—choosing to separate your faith from your community in order to maintain your preferred way of life. Rather than engaging your city with your faith, you keep your faith to yourself. You are taking your personal relationship with Jesus Christ, something that was meant to be public, and turning it into something it was never meant to be, namely a private affair.

Christianity calls for the death of selfishness. More than that, Christianity calls for the death of self. A relationship with Jesus is built only as we die to ourselves and enter into a new life where Jesus and the concerns of others become our chief concern (Phil. 2:1–8, 20–21). Ironically, once you die to yourself, you begin to experience the life God created you to live—a purposeful, fulfilling life of using your strengths and gifts for the benefit and flourishing of others. This is a key discovery that all Christians are meant to make: we flourish as we live our lives for the flourishing of others.

What's problematic about either abandoning or privatizing the Christian worldview is that both approaches get it wrong. The Christian worldview calls for a reversal of values, a death of self, that leaves no room for being evasive or privatizing what's meant to be deeply public, namely, faith in Jesus.

An important passage for Christians living in the city is Philippians 2. Here we find the apostle Paul's words to a group of Christians figuring out how to live in the diverse, pluralistic, and strategic city of Philippi—a leading city in Macedonia and the Roman Empire. Paul combats selfishness by calling believers in Philippi to forget about themselves and be most concerned with the interests of others: "Do nothing from selfish ambition or conceit, but in humility count others more significant than yourselves. Let each of you look not only to his own interests, but also to the interests of others" (Phil. 2:3–4). Paul follows these imperatives by going even further, asking the Christians in Philippi to have the mind of Christ, to approach their city in a similar manner to Christ's approach to his incarnation and earthly ministry:

> Have this mind among yourselves, which is yours in Christ Jesus, who, though he was in the form of God, did not count equality with God a thing to be grasped, but emptied himself, by taking the form of a servant, being born in the likeness of men. And being found in human form, he humbled himself by becoming obedient to the point of death, even death on a cross. (Phil. 2:5–8)

Jesus took on human flesh for the sake of ministry. Paul asks the citizens of Philippi to adopt a similar mind-set, to be deeply concerned for the welfare of others in their community and city.

CONTEXTUALIZING YOUR WORLDVIEW IN THE CITY

Rather than abandoning or concealing our faith, Jesus calls us to contextualize our Christian worldview in our cities. The call to carefully contextualize the gospel is Jesus's command writ large: "You shall love your neighbor as yourself" (Matt. 19:19). It is the best way to engage and love our cities. Cities are simply places full of neighbors, places with a higher and more diverse concentration of people than found elsewhere. Think of your city as a place teeming with neighbors whom you are called to know, love, and engage with the gospel. What is beautiful and what is broken in your city is a product of the long history of good and evil committed by the inhabitants of the city, good and evil that have meshed together to create the dominant cultural motifs of your city.

You should contextualize your worldview to your city the same way you would go about contextualizing your faith to an individual neighbor: listen first, speak second.

To love your neighbor intelligently and to share your faith credibly, you must first understand your neighbor. You must learn your neighbor's history, values, fears, dreams, and mode of operation. Once you begin to learn your neighbors, you have information by which you can most effectively love and communicate to them. This rule of relationship also governs our relationship to our cities. Contextualization in the city is essentially the task of getting to know your city's story in order to find the points at which that narrative overlaps or differs with the gospel. It is obtaining the information you need to most effectively love and communicate to your city.

Who is your city? This is a question asked by Richard Florida—it's actually the title of his book, *Who's Your City? How the Creative Economy Is Making Where to Live the Most Important Decision of Your Life.*[15] Using the pronoun "who" in the title, Florida personifies the cities of our world, arguing that every city has a unique personality that we must understand if we are to thrive in the city. Florida's thesis is important for us—we must understand the unique personalities of our cities in order to contextualize the gospel and best serve our cities.

So, who's your city? Do you know your city's personality?

Again, the best way to learn your city is to follow the same tactics you would use for learning about your neighbor: ask questions, listen, learn.

We like working with five questions for discovering the DNA of cities. We could certainly utilize many more questions for diagnosing the heartbeat of a city—the more questions you ask the more you learn—but we've found that these five offer an excellent starting point for understanding the city. What follows is incomplete. We realize that cities are diverse, home to thousands of subcultures that don't fit generalizations, and we could write whole books in response to each of these five questions. Nevertheless, we've found that thoughtful engagement with these five questions gives people a critical foundation for understanding the basic dynamics of their city and for thinking through how to best live out their Christian life.

In the sections that follow, we use Silicon Valley/San Jose as a sample city. Silicon Valley and San Jose are almost interchangeable terms. San Jose is the tenth largest city in America and is known as "The Capital of Silicon Valley," a region with its epicenter in San Jose, but that extends beyond the city limits and is framed by the borders of Santa Clara County.[16]

Question 1: What Is Your City's History?

One of the characteristics of healthy cities is their unique ability continually to reinvent themselves around the ideas and innovation of their people. The powerful combination of clustered density and connective diversity not only produces amazing culture and technology, it also sustains cities through dramatic changes in the historical, economic, and social climate. The story of San Jose is one of continual reinvention and regeneration.

San Jose is the oldest city in California. It was founded in 1777 as California's first civilian settlement.[17] The early settlers of San Jose often referred to their city as the "Garden City"[18] because the crops they planted grew and flourished in the city's good soil and temperate climate. This was a prophetic name for the city that's grown to become "The Capital of Silicon Valley," a slice of land in Northern California that exerts an exponential worldwide influence.

Silicon Valley has a rich history of entrepreneurship. The story begins in the latter half of the eighteenth century with Felipe de Neve, the Spaniard appointed to build the first civilian settlement in California.[19] Neve started "the new pueblo of San Jose de Guadalupe" with a group of fourteen men and their families.[20] In 1848, California joined the United States after a series of events that included Mexico's secession from Spain, multiple skirmishes, a war, and a treaty between the United States and Mexico. Though San Jose became a city seventy years before California joined the United States, it was chosen as the state's first capital.

By the time California became a state, Silicon Valley had already reinvented itself. Originally the economy of Silicon Valley revolved around cattle—exporting and selling the valuable rawhide and tallow from California livestock. This changed in 1848 with the California Gold Rush. With rapid population growth in Northern California, the need for food in the gold country spiked, as did food prices, and the land of Silicon Valley shifted from being used for raising cattle to being used mostly for growing wheat, eventually making California the nation's leading wheat producer. Next came the city's third major move. Discovering an abundance of underground water, Santa Clara Valley shifted (seemingly overnight) to an economy built around fruit orchards. Before Silicon Valley was called "Silicon Valley," it was called "The Garden of the World," producing apricots, peaches, cherries, and a variety of other fruits that were exported worldwide. With the advent of silicon chip production, the city entered its fourth major entrepreneurial cycle, earning the new name, "Silicon Valley." A city once inhabited by cattle ranchers, then wheat farmers, and then fruit farmers is now largely inhabited by entrepreneurs of a different sort who hail from all over the world.[21]

While San Jose is an old city by California standards, it's a very young city by world standards. Take Paris for example. For over two thousand years Paris has been a thriving city, surviving countless economic and political paradigm shifts. Paris is the most visited city in the world.[22] The history of Paris is much longer and involves many more plot twists than Silicon Valley. We're not suggesting you must become a historical scholar on your city, but you should know the major narrative threads of your city's history in order to best understand who your city is today. Being a historian of your city will inform your interpretation and assessment of the things that drive your city in the present. Silicon Valley makes more sense once you understand its entrepreneurial and diverse beginnings, just as Paris makes more sense once you understand that as early as 52 BC (when the Paris basin was conquered by the Romans), the city quickly became a cultural center with an amphitheater, forum, temples, baths, palaces, and businesses. The roots of a city help you understand the current makeup of a city. What is your city's history?

Question 2: What Are Your City's Values?

Most businesses and nonprofits have a set of core values that shape their DNA and culture. Cities also have core values; the only difference would be that a city's values are generally assumed rather than stated. Six words immediately come to mind when thinking about the core values of Silicon Valley: innovation, entrepreneurialism, work, speed, accomplishment, and wealth.

Innovation and entrepreneurialism pervade Silicon Valley. We saw this spirit in the history of the city, and it is what Silicon Valley is known for worldwide. Silicon Valley is a place to start things. It would be difficult to connect meaningfully with Silicon Valley residents without understanding this deep-seated value of entrepreneurship which shapes how people think, feel, and pursue their future.

Work. People don't move to Silicon Valley to rest. People move there to work. Work is a central value in most cities, but it is king in Silicon Valley. Work is valued in a different way in Silicon Valley than it is in San Diego, where the lifestyle is much more laid-back.

This makes *speed* a key value. Reid Hoffman, venture capitalist and cofounder of LinkedIn, says: "Silicon Valley has two speeds: full speed ahead and not going anywhere."[23] Things move fast, or they don't move at all.

Accomplishment. Silicon Valley has a type A personality. It's a city full of achievers and overachievers. It's common for six-year-old boys to have a private soccer coach (in hopes of earning a soccer scholarship someday) and for seven-year-old girls to have private tutors in several different subjects (in hopes of earning an academic scholarship someday). It's no accident that the university best known for the combination of academic and athletic excellence, Stanford University, is located in Silicon Valley. It's a region known not for its talk, but for its action—for making things happen, getting things done, and accomplishing goals.

Finally, *wealth* is deeply valued in Silicon Valley. Wealth is often the objective of many start-ups in Silicon Valley, but it's also a requirement to be able to afford to live in this part of the world. Edward Glaeser writes:

> In the expensive areas on America's coasts, demand is robust, because of high incomes and pleasures. . . . California's Santa Clara County, Silicon Valley, has a splendid Mediterranean climate and incomes that are 60 percent above the U.S. average. Unsurprisingly, people will pay plenty to live there. Between 2005 and 2007, average housing prices in the county were close to $800,000, more than four times the U.S. average. Prices have dropped since then, but according to recent sales data, the San Jose metropolitan area, which includes Santa Clara County, remained the most expensive place in the continental United States in the second quarter of 2009.[24]

Wealth must be valued, to some degree, simply to enable one to live in the San Jose metropolitan area.

All world-class cities with high creative, innovative, and technological indexes will likely share similar values. In this way, Silicon Valley has much more in common with geographically distant cities like New York, Tokyo, and Boston than fellow California cities like Sacramento and San Diego.[25] Whatever the case, until you understand your city's values, winsomely engaging it with the gospel of Jesus Christ will be a formidable task.

What are your city's values?

Question 3: What Are Your City's Dreams?

In a word, Silicon Valley dreams of influence. The aspiration of Silicon Valley is to shape the world, and to create technology, innovation, and business that will positively impact culture. Las Vegas is a city with a very different dream. The city's mantra reads, "What happens in Vegas, stays in Vegas." Las Vegas is driven by a dream to be a pleasure city, where traditional inhibitions and consequences magically disappear. What happens in Vegas might stay in Vegas, but what happens in Silicon Valley impacts the world. Las Vegas's vision is to import, Silicon Valley's vision is to export.

What are your city's dreams?

Question 4: What Are Your City's Fears?

A city's fears represent the counterpart of its values. Silicon Valley fears the status quo (the opposite of innovation and entrepreneurialism), rest (the opposite of work), lack of forward movement (the opposite of speed), mediocrity and failure (the opposite of achievement), and limited options (the opposite of wealth). By understanding these deeply felt fears, one understands why Silicon Valley's residents were so deeply rattled by the dot-com crash of 2000—it wasn't only that money was lost, but the experience of having one's values threatened and worst fears realized. In contrast, modern-day Jerusalem, Kabul, and Cairo have very different fears—these are cities seemingly ever-teetering on the brink of revolution or war. A city's fears say almost as much about it as its idols do. If you know your city's vulnerabilities, you will be able to apply the comforting truths of the gospel directly to the hearts of your neighbors.

What are your city's fears?

Question 5: What Is Your City's Ethos?

A city's ethos is shaped by its unique geography, history, and climate. Silicon Valley's mode of operation is car-based and casual.

San Jose grew up once the automobile was already a staple technology in America. As a result, Silicon Valley is geographically expansive and navigated largely by car: [26]

> In some ways Silicon Valley looks completely different from any
> older city. It is built almost entirely around the car. While there

are some areas, particularly in downtown Palo Alto, where you can walk a few pleasant blocks to get an ice cream or buy a book, feet are generally useless for getting from one company to another. A few companies, like Google, run their own bus services, but public transportation is minimal. Only 3.7 percent of the people living in Santa Clara county take mass transit to work.[27]

Silicon Valley operates much differently than San Francisco. San Francisco is hedged by water on three sides, encompasses a geography of just seven miles (north-south) by seven miles (east-west), is much more densely populated than San Jose (even though San Jose is the bigger city with a much larger population), and is navigated, largely, by public transit and walking. Nevertheless, Silicon Valley functions like a dense city:

> It's true that Silicon Valley looks like the West Coast antithesis of Jane Jacob's Greenwich Village. And yet, I'd argue [that] the culture of Silicon Valley manages to replicate the essential function of a dense city, which is to foster a diversity of interactions and knowledge spill-overs. . . . Silicon Valley has managed for decades to foster the sort of cross-cutting connections that are essential for innovation. Because the San Jose area has traditionally consisted of small and fledgling startups, these firms have traditionally had to collaborate on projects and share engineers. As a result, it wasn't uncommon for a scientist at Cisco to be friends with someone at Oracle, or for a co-founder of Intel to offer management advice to a young executive at Apple. These networks often led to high employee turnover, as people jumped from project to project. In the 1980s, for instance, the average tenure at a Silicon Valley company was less than two years. . . . the creativity of a city depends on our constantly mixing and mingling.[28]

Silicon Valley is also casual. Dress is casual, language is casual, and the feel of the city is casual. Much of this is likely due to the weather: "Silicon Valley . . . has arguably the best climate in the United States."[29] People dress casually in the city's pleasant weather—venture capitalists, executives at Apple and Google, CEOs of small start-ups, and college freshmen all dress fairly similar. The entrepreneurial icon of Silicon Valley, the late Steve Jobs, dressed in jeans, tennis shoes, and what was essentially a long-sleeved black T-shirt. And, true to Silicon Valley's casual language, he wasn't known or addressed as "Mr. Jobs," people simply called him "Steve." Because Silicon Valley runs on decentralized start-ups and innovation, it lends itself to this casualness. The ethos is different in Boston where older, more centralized corporations lend themselves to formality and tradition in language and dress.

We dress and speak quite differently in our different churches and cities. Stephen preaches in center-city Boston with a jacket and tie, speaking to a highly educated and well-dressed congregation. Justin preaches in Silicon Valley in jeans, speaking to a well-educated yet very informal congregation clothed in jeans, T-shirts, and flip-flops. Yet both Boston and Silicon Valley are high-pressure cities, where time is among people's most precious commodity. The mode of operation in Boston, Silicon Valley, Tokyo, and Shanghai is quite similar—fast-paced—where people are incessantly busy. Yet Mexico City and Paris operate differently—the pace is slower. Discovering the ethos of your city will give you insight into how your city defines comfort, community, status, and honor. Knowing this will greatly assist you in contextualizing the unchanging gospel for your unique urban context.

What is your city's ethos?

MOVING FORWARD WITH CONTEXTUALIZATION

We encourage you to take the time to ask these questions of your city. This is best done in community. Gather others in your community and work through the five city questions. Converse with people in your city, read your city's newspapers, spend time walking the streets of your city and visiting its establishments, study your city's history, and sit with these questions for a season. Do so prayerfully. Contextualization is a crucial skill to develop, particularly in cities:

> Skill in contextualization is one of the keys to effective ministry today. In particular, churches in urban and cultural centers must be

exceptionally sensitive to issues of contextualization, because it is largely there that a society's culture is being forged and is taking new directions. It is also a place where multiple human cultures live together in uneasy tension, so cultural compounds are more complex and blended there.[30]

Addressing how to go about the work of contextualization, Jonathan Dodson states what many seem to have forgotten, the simple and organic nature of contextualization: "Spend more time with people. . . . Spend time with . . . your fellow citizens, your neighbors. Ask them good questions. . . . The more you know and love them, the more you will be able to share the gospel in a way that makes sense, that strips away misunderstandings of the gospel and slides in truly good news."[31] Again, cities are people. Cities matter because people matter. And as you listen to and learn from the people of your city, you'll discover that the work and skill of contextualization can become both a natural and an exciting experience.

Once we wrestle with these questions, we can begin contextualizing our life and ministry in the city. This was the practice of the apostle Paul. Acts 17 chronicles how Paul took an inventory of the history, values, dreams, and fears of the city of Athens before speaking to the Athenians about God. Paul spoke to and engaged the people of Athens in a way that both embraced and challenged the Athenian personality.

Richard Florida wrote *Who's Your City?* so that people could choose the city personality that best fits their needs. In this vision, one moves to the city as a means of self-fulfillment and -realization. The Bible gives Christians a different call into cities. Because we derive our identity and fulfillment from Christ, our purpose in understanding the personality of a city is never self-centered. Rather, we seek to contextualize so that we can serve our cities, so that we can do ministry that will help them to flourish.

This is our next task, to explore how contextualization in the city informs our ministry in the city.

DISCUSSION QUESTIONS

1. Do you tend to lean toward abandoning or privatizing your worldview? Is it easier for you to be "in the world" or "not of the world"? If you lean toward accommodating the idols of your city, what are some of the ways that you can ensure that you are not overcome by the idolatrous paradigms of your city? If you tend to be separatistic, brainstorm a few ways that you could engage the world without succumbing to its idols.

2. What would it look like for you to strike a balance and rightly contextualize the gospel in your setting? Would the way that you use your time and resources look different?

3. Can you describe the idols of your city? How are your personal idols similar to or different from the idols of your city? How does the gospel uniquely address your city's unique idols? How might you present the gospel to a person who is clearly trapped in your city's cycle of idolatry?

4. If someone asked you to describe the history of your city, what would you tell him or her? Do you have a working understanding of how your city came to be what it is? What does your city's history tell you about the people who live there and how might you more effectively communicate the gospel to them?

5. What are the values of your city? On what basis are the people of your city judged? What does your city strive toward? What are some of the points of overlap with the gospel? What values and dreams does your city have that the gospel exposes as false?

Chapter 5

THE STORY LINE
OF THE CITY

[There] are social idols that capture the life of the city . . .
overarching sinful narratives on which people rely. We
have to exegete them. We have to spot them out. We have
to capture their core values, their history, their attractions,
and the shape they have given to the city. . . . We have to
grasp spiritually the theological skyline of the city.[1]

Leonardo de Chirico

The Gospels record two instances where Jesus shed tears. One occasion was over the death of a friend. As he felt grief over Lazarus's death, "Jesus wept" (John 11:35). The other occasion involves Jesus's heart for a city. As Jesus approached the city of Jerusalem, the place where he would soon be betrayed, crucified, and buried, the Gospel of Luke records, "When he drew near and saw the city, he wept over it" (Luke 19:41).[2]

This is telling. At the center of the Christian faith stands a Savior who wept over a city he loved. Jesus was emotionally involved with this city—both its beauty and its brokenness deeply affected him. Jesus reveals God's heart for cities, a heart that is deeply concerned for the welfare of cities and the well-being of the people who populate them. We know that we're gaining a sense of God's heart for our city when we experience what Jesus experienced—being emotionally moved over the condition of our city. Ministry in the city cannot happen merely with an analytical posture, simply seeing our cities as a project to be improved, fixed, or worked on. Remember, cities are people. The call to do ministry in the city is an extrapolation of the great commandment to love our neighbor. In order to love your neighbor well, your heart must be engaged—you must truly care about your neighbor, not approaching your neighbor as a project to fix or a task to complete. And to love your city well you must truly care about your city, you must ask God to give you his heart and vision for your city.

Do this. Before reading about ministry in the city, start with repentance and prayer. Repent of ways you have either abandoned or privatized your Christian faith in your city. Then, ask God to give you his heart for your city. Meditate on some of the passages we've highlighted throughout this book (review the key passages in chap. 3) and ask God to give you a fresh sense of calling and concern for your city.

THE COMPLETION OF YOUR CITY'S STORY LINE

Every city has a story. Once you've worked through the five city questions from chapter 4—your city's history, values, dreams, fears, and ethos—you can piece together your city's narrative. The baseline story is the overarching belief system that drives how a city functions. Knowing, engaging, and challenging this story line is the next step in contextualization and the key to doing ministry in the city.

This is what the apostle Paul did. What made Paul's city ministry so effective was that he understood the deepest hopes and idolatries of cities. Therefore, he was able to declare and demonstrate the gospel in such a way that a city's hopes were reinterpreted and its idols were challenged. Whether he was speaking to a Jewish or a Gentile audience, it was typical for Paul to enter a city and address, disrupt, and retell a city's story line with the good news of Jesus. This generally led to both a citywide uproar and the planting of a strong church. Paul's ministry method was both simple and subversive. And it was effective. Note Paul's hope-reinforcing and idolatry-challenging method of restabilizing a city's story line with a Jewish audience in Antioch of Pisidia (Acts 13), a Gentile audience in Lystra (Acts 14), a predominantly Gentile audience in Philippi (Acts 16), and a mixed audience in

Thessalonica (Acts 17), Athens (Acts 17), Corinth (Acts 18), Ephesus (Acts 19), and Jerusalem (Acts 21).[3]

We are convinced that the thinness of some Christian discipleship and ministry in cities is a result of not fully embracing Paul's contextual approach. We have not learned to retell our city's story line with the gospel. Once we learn to do this, we believe deep ministry can begin to happen in our cities.[4] Three steps are involved in this process: know your city's story, challenge your city's story, and retell your city's story.[5]

KNOW YOUR CITY'S STORY

We can't minister well to our neighbor until we know our neighbor. And we can't minister well to our city until we know our city. "We must free ourselves from our tendency to see cities as their buildings, and remember that the real city is made of flesh, not concrete."[6] The five city questions give you the data points you need to piece together the story that your city believes. Again, we offer a disclaimer. We acknowledge that in every city there are countless subcultures that cling to diverse narratives to make sense and meaning out of life. "Global city centers are complex salad bowls of all worldviews."[7] Nevertheless, we believe it is both true and helpful to see that one overarching big story line tends to drive and define the life of our cities. A city's inhabitants can be either consciously or subconsciously aware of this narrative. More often than not, our relationship to our city's story line is like a fish's relationship to water: we're so immersed in it that we don't notice it until it is threatened. The first-century urban world in which Paul ministered was quite similar to our world today: pluralistic and diverse. Yet despite the diversity and lack of a monolithic culture, Paul was still able to discern and address a city's overarching story such that his ministry touched a major nerve throughout the city.

We find it helpful to summarize a city's story with one word or a sentence. Doing so gives you a handle for quickly understanding the hopes and idols at work in your city. What follows is an attempt to summarize the diverse story lines of thirty of our world's cities. We do this at the risk of arrogance and ignorance (we live in only two of these cities, though we've spent time in many of them) and offense (you might live in these cities and disagree with our diagnosis). At the very least, reading this diverse list will give you a starting point for thinking in this vein.

Boston: Knowledge	Austin: Independence
Silicon Valley: Success[8]	Tokyo: Competitive
Seoul: Competition	Conformity[11]
Manila: Opportunity	Geneva: Peace
Washington, DC: Power	Tehran: Power
Hong Kong:	Lagos: Progress[12]
Entrepreneurship	Boulder: Adventure
Phnom Penh: Reformation	Singapore: Order
San Francisco: Equality	Los Angeles: Image
Sydney: Pleasure	Dubai: Success
Beijing: Politics	Moscow: Power
Paris: Romance	San Diego: Health
Oklahoma City: Family[9]	Dublin: Tradition
London: Influence	Detroit: Hope[13]
Las Vegas: Pleasure	Cairo: Revolution
Bangalore: Innovation[10]	New York: Success

Before doing ministry in a city, Paul knew its story. Putting together what we know from first-century urban history and Paul's speeches in the book of Acts, you could say that Paul discerned the story of some of the cities in which he did ministry as follows:

Jerusalem: Tradition
Rome: Power
Athens: Knowledge
Ephesus: Religion

When you put together the history, values, dreams, fears, and ethos of a city, you can discern the overarching story line that drives how a city operates and how its inhabitants live. Ancient Rome was driven by a story of ultimate power. Modern-day Silicon Valley views success as the key to life. Presently, "freedom" summarizes the plotline of Johannesburg, a city eager to right the wrongs of apartheid. Just thirty years ago, this was certainly not the case. Johannesburg has been called "the most transformed city in Africa."[14] This should encourage us to believe that our cities can also change. Things don't have to stay the way they are.

How would you describe the prevailing voice of your city?

What are its idols and dreams?

How should this sense of your city's story shape how you live, work, worship, and witness in your city?

CHALLENGE YOUR CITY'S STORY

The next step is to destabilize your city's story. Contextualized city ministry discerns the idols at the foundation of a city's story and skillfully confronts them. Culturally engaged city ministry also discerns the deep hopes at play in a city's ruling narrative, setting you up to retell it with the ultimate hope that is found in the gospel.

Scripture constantly warns us of the danger and destruction caused by the worship of anything other than God. What follows are among the strongest passages speaking against the danger of idolatry. What's often missed is that many of these passages speak to the idolatry of a city and the consequences idolatry brings to a city. Prayerfully read these passages while thinking about the idolatry at work in your city.

> Do not turn to idols or make for yourselves any gods of cast metal: I am the LORD your God. (Lev. 19:4)

> And they abandoned the house of the LORD, the God of their fathers, and served the Asherim and the idols. And wrath came upon Judah and Jerusalem for this guilt of theirs. (2 Chron. 24:18)

> I am the LORD; that is my name;
> my glory I give to no other,
> nor my praise to carved idols. (Isa. 42:8)

Your altars shall become desolate, and your incense altars shall be broken, and I will cast down your slain before your idols. And I will lay the dead bodies of the people of Israel before their idols, and I will scatter your bones around your altars. Wherever you dwell, the cities shall be waste and the high places ruined, so that your altars will be waste and ruined, your idols broken and destroyed . . . your works wiped out. (Ezek. 6:4–6)

Those who pay regard to vain idols
    forsake their hope of steadfast love. (Jonah 2:8)

Now while Paul was waiting for them at Athens, his spirit was provoked within him as he saw that the city was full of idols. (Acts 17:16)

All cities are centers of worship, and urban dwellers are some of the most passionate, driven worshipers on earth. The issue is not worship. The issue is the false gods that garner our affection, devotion, and praise. In some cities of our world people are bowing down to gods of cast metal (Lev. 19:4), but in most of our cities idolatry has become modernized. People bow down to money, power, image, approval, success, fame, comfort, control, etc. What unfortunately happens in many of our cities is shallow ministry that simply adds Jesus to existing idolatries. People hear the gospel as a call to merely add Jesus to their lives, keeping their idolatry—the central orbit of their life—fully intact. The linchpin of the apostle Paul's life-changing ministry was his ability to directly challenge a city's idolatry, calling people to repent and leave behind their false gods and to begin worshiping the living God. Recalling his ministry in Thessalonica, a city with a population of over one hundred thousand and the capital of the Roman province of Macedonia,[15] Paul writes: "For they themselves report concerning us the kind of reception we had among you, and *how you turned to God from idols to serve the living and true God*" (1 Thess. 1:9). The ancient Thessalonians left behind their idols in order to worship God. If we don't challenge our city's story, there will be no leaving behind of idols, just mixed worship of both God and idols.

If ministry in the city is not contextualized to challenge a city's unique idolatry, then our ministry will be shallow and unsubstantial. If a city's false hopes are not exposed, we will find it difficult to demonstrate how Jesus meets the deepest needs of a community's inhabitants. Jesus must be shown as the one who offers resolution to unresolved plotlines and completion to fragmented narratives by way of his substitutionary work on the cross.[16] To do this, we must know our city's idols. The problem is that most of us are blind to *our* idols, in the same way that most cities are blind to their idols.

Everyone has to live for something, and if that something isn't the one true God, it will be a counterfeit hope. A false god is anything that is more important to you than God. Therefore, you can turn even very good things into idolatrous things. You can turn *good* gifts like family, success, acceptance, money, aspirations, etc., into a *god* thing—into something you worship and place at the center of your life.

This is what sin is. Sin is building your life and ultimate meaning on anything other than God. Do you know the idols you are prone to worship? Do you know the idols your city worships? At our churches we talk about four root idols that often take prominence in the human heart:

Control. You know you have a control idol if your greatest nightmare is uncertainty.

Approval. You know you have an approval idol if your greatest nightmare is rejection.

Comfort. You know you have a comfort idol if your greatest nightmare is stress/demands.

Power. You know you have a power idol if your greatest nightmare is humiliation.[17]

Here's what you need to know about the idol that you love: it doesn't love you back. False gods don't love you. Idols don't keep their promises. Anything you worship and build your life on other than God will suck the life out of you and destroy you. The key to challenging your city's idolatry is to expose this reality—that idols don't deliver, but in fact destroy.

A relationship with Jesus starts when you identify and turn from your idols. Notice what Jesus was always doing with people during his ministry—he was constantly identifying and challenging their idols, calling people to turn from their false objects of worship in order to follow and worship him. This, then, became exactly the practice of the apostle Paul, who structured his ministry and his message to challenge directly a city's prevailing idolatry. In order to address idols at the individual level, he chose to address them at the city level. Our individual idolatries are deeply intertwined with the false worship at work in our cities.

Most city dwellers think that freedom is found in casting off all restraint and believing that they are omnicompetent to rule their own lives. This is the reason many move to the city in the first place—to escape restraints. Our explorational friend from chapter 2 has lived in four cities in four years because he believes that each city offers him an opportunity to become more fully realized, to experience life to the fullest, and to break free from traditional, moralistic constraints. Unfortunately, he is blind to the reality that he is being ruled by his false gods, and is caught in a synthetic, life-destroying story. Idols make poor rulers. They tyrannize.

Until we identify the idols in our lives, we will feel enslaved, exhausted, and unhappy. This will be our experience until we are confronted with the freedom, rest, and satisfaction that come only through Jesus. He is the one Ruler who will love you even when you fail him. Your idols don't do that. The overworked, dissatisfied people in your city need to hear this. Jesus is the one Master who loved you when you were at your worst, who substituted his life for yours, and who reigns over your life with perfect wisdom, power, and love. The self-defined, self-ruled, self-possessed people in your city need to hear this. He's the one Master you can trust. He's the only Master who can give you freedom.

What we expressed in these last few paragraphs is the simple yet deep ministry of challenging your city's story. Part of your city's story is built upon honorable hopes that need to be affirmed (this we will address in the third step: retell your city's story), and part of your city's story is built upon dangerous idolatry that needs to be exposed and confronted. This middle step calls for you to destabilize your city's story in a way that addresses both its hopes and its idolatries.

This is not a light exercise, but will require uncommon love, vulnerability, tenacity, suffering, and passion to see people set free and Jesus's name lifted high. It will also require something more than sociological or intellectual analysis. Leonardo de Chirico, pastor of *Chiesa Evangelica Breccia Di Roma* in Rome, reminds us that destabilizing your city's story is essentially a spiritual task:

> Identifying the idols of the city takes place in the untamed context of spiritual warfare. Those who are engaged in mapping the idolatry of the city know that this process is not simply a rational, cognitive, scholarly engagement. It is first and foremost a spiritual battle involving spiritual discernment. Acts 17:16 tells us that in Athens, Paul was "greatly distressed to see that the city was full of idols." He was spiritually disturbed. Unless we feel—we sense and experience—that sense of distress, uneasiness, and spiritual discomfort, all talk about idols will be meaningless. To identify the idols of the city . . . is a matter of spiritual discernment in the context of spiritual warfare. It is a matter of having our spiritual senses geared to the spiritual condition of the city. . . .
>
> It is altogether different from a romantic love for the city. It is different from a naïve approach to urbanization. Of course, cities are to be loved, but unless we experience that sense of spiritual angst for the city, that sense of unrest, that sting that punches us and makes us vulnerable, we will not be able to map the idols of the city. . . . Willingness to pay the cost of spiritual participation is an essential ingredient towards identifying idols. Identifying the idols of the city requires spiritual suffering and pain.[18]

You must search for the soul of your city just as Paul did in Athens and just as Jesus did in Jerusalem—with a provoked spirit and tears in your eyes.

Let's use Dubai as an example of challenging your city's story. People move to, live in, and work in this global city in order to lay claim to its story line of success. As a business hub, Dubai is chasing success through the oil, real estate, construction, financial, and tourism industries. The city is currently ranked first in the world for luxury housing,[19] and has a list of ornate tourist attractions that reads like something out of another world.[20] Dubai boasts the tallest building in the world, Burj Khalifa, a skyscraper that reaches 2,723 feet. Needless to say, Dubai is not shy in revealing its twin idolatries—money and power.

Located in the United Arab Emirates, Dubai is a Muslim city in a Muslim country centered in the Muslim hub of the world. In this context, the ministry of challenging the city's idols of money and power is immensely difficult. In 2008 Dave and Gloria Furman moved their family from Texas to plant a church in downtown Dubai. Gloria offers a glimpse into the suffering they've experienced and discoveries they've made doing ministry in Dubai:

> In the middle of a city in the Middle East there is a cement house on a street without a name that is filled with memories of grief and hope. In that unlikely place the idols of our city, the idols of my heart, and the comforting presence of God became real to me.
>
> In 2008 we moved our family to Dubai to plant a church. We never expected our first season in the city to rock our worlds like it did. It was like the stars aligned in Shakespearean style to make our lives miserable. Our 18-month-old daughter settled into full-blown culture shock and her cheerful personality wilted like a cut rose.
>
> I was no different. I entered the second trimester of pregnancy and instead of feeling better physically I began to feel nauseous and weak. I didn't go outside for fear of gawking neighbors and the flies and the smell. Our house was next to a dumpster where people discarded animal carcasses from the sacrifices they conducted. I could barely read the language much less speak it. I missed my friends, our teammates were delayed, and God seemed so distant. The spiri-

tual oppression was rank like the acrid incense that rose to a god who has no hands to help and no power to save.

Then my husband's arms, which had recently undergone major surgery, got worse. Dave could no longer lift a metal fork to eat, button his shirt, write Arabic, or pick up his Bible. His arms felt like they were on fire. I begged God for relief in our circumstances, and it didn't come. I remember lying awake in bed watching Dave pace the floor in agonizing pain. I worried about him. I drew a strange comfort from the fact that he couldn't drive the car and potentially drive off out of desperation for change. And the thought occurred to me that we had made a big mistake. Dubai worships money and power. These idols are written across the skyscraper skyline of our city and across the faces of the people. For the first time I felt the allure of these idols (If only I had more power?). My God seemed distant and the idols of our city seemed to offer relief.

Then the Holy Spirit spoke in my mind Romans 8:32, "He who did not spare His own Son but gave Him up for us all, how will He not also with Him graciously give us all things?" God wanted me to remember that my hope was not in how I could fix my circumstances. God, in His kindness, wanted to show me that my hope lay solely in the never-quitting zeal of the grace of Jesus Christ.

I didn't get "un-stuck" that night . . . it took some time. But there in the midst of the darkness, my heart caught a fresh glimpse of the gospel. And I knew that God had not abandoned me, or my city. He is about something far bigger than me, my family, and money and power. He is making himself famous through weak people discovering and proclaiming the strength of his Son who hung bleeding on a cross.

Six months later we left that house still in pain and still disabled. But instead of banking our happiness in health and strength, we purposed to lean heavily on the one who suffered the greatest pain as he bore our sin to give us the ability to live. Only the wisdom of this gospel can mystify our city's impotent idols—and mine. Our crisis came at the same time as our city's crisis, a major economic and property-market crash that left much of our city in debt and disillusioned. This was one of the best things that could've happened to our city. All of a sudden, people saw through the idols. Money and power looked impotent now, like false gods. I discovered two things at the same time: my idols don't satisfy me and Dubai's idols don't satisfy Dubai, we were both created for something bigger and better—knowing and worshiping the one true God.[21]

Ministry in the city will look different for all of us. But it ought to always look something like Dave and Gloria's story in Dubai—we confront the idolatry of our city while our own idolatries are simultaneously challenged. When you pursue this kind of ministry, you discover that the city doesn't merely need you, you also need the city. As we rub shoulders with the people and idols of our city, our own idols, blind spots, and prejudices are exposed. "One of the biggest barriers to effective contextualization is the invisibility of our own cultural assumptions."[22] It's not just the city's story that's being challenged—the diversity of the city will also challenge and destabilize your story. In this way, God sets both you and your city up to experience the gospel in a fresh way as it reorders your hopes and ties up the loose ends of an unsatisfying story.

RETELL YOUR CITY'S STORY

Nearly three centuries ago, author Samuel Johnson famously declared: "When a man is tired of London, he is tired of life; for there is in London all that life can afford."[23] Johnson articulated a popular sentiment of the time, especially among London's upwardly mobile—that London was the greatest city in the world, a place of unending delights. Eighteenth-century Londoners sought prosperity and flourishing in their city; they lived under a city story line of ambition, abundance, and progress. Ministry to Samuel Johnson and eighteenth-century London certainly would have included challenging some of the idols at work in such a boastful statement, yet there is much to affirm in Johnson's boast.

The gospel doesn't eradicate a city's story, but it brings completeness to it. Once a city's story has been challenged, it must be retold. And it must be retold to show that a city's story can only find a happy ending through Jesus's substitutionary resolution and completion of the themes of the city's story line. The gospel resolves the thickening tension in the city's narrative, and shows that resolution, relief, and rest are to be found only in Jesus Christ.

The error we often make in the city is announcing the gospel without ever connecting it to the hopes and the idols of the city. Though Samuel Johnson was certainly guilty of some idolatry, his encouragement to enjoy a flourishing urban environment is commendable. Eighteenth-century London was the undisputed cultural, economic, religious, educational, literary, artistic, and political center of the nation—and the biggest city in all of Europe.[24] Ministry to Johnson's London would have needed to retell the great London story, showing that the noble pursuit of deep human flourishing and cultural development could only find true completion in Jesus and the city that is to come. Great cities like London do contain most of what this world has to offer. Much of it is wonderful, but it leaves us wanting. God's redemptive plan for this world includes the promise of a heavenly city that does not leave us wanting, a place where our insatiable longings will be fulfilled completely. The gospel announces more than a wonderful plan for one's individual life, it also announces a wonderful plan for the world. Retelling the story of eighteenth-century London would mean pointing Londoners to the Savior that truly satisfies and the great city that is to come. And ultimately, it is this true satisfaction in Christ that frees us to enjoy the culture of cities like London, without expecting our cities to satisfy the human heart.

This is what Paul did in Athens. While challenging the city's idols, he also affirmed the city's longing for transcendence and meaning. Paul even quoted from pagan poets in order to establish the existence of the one true God, so that he could point the city toward him. Paul retold the Athenian story, announcing that their story—their great hopes and dreams—could find a happy ending only in God. For only "in him we live and move and have our being" (Acts 17:28).

Paul never approached two different cities in the same way. He knew that each city had a different culture, a different story that needed to be uniquely addressed by the unchanging gospel. We believe that one of the most important components of city ministry is restabilizing a city's story with the gospel. If we are unable to speak to the deepest aspirations, longings, hopes, and fears of our cities, we are missing significant opportunities for making gospel connections:

> The same impulse that makes us want our books to have a plot makes us want our lives to have a plot. We need to feel that we are getting somewhere, making progress. There is something in us that is not satisfied with a merely psychological explanation of our lives. It doesn't do justice to our conviction that we are on some kind of journey or quest, that there must be some deeper meaning to our lives than whether we feel good about ourselves. Only people who have lost the sense of adventure, mystery, and romance worry about their self-esteem. And at that point what they need is not a good therapist, but a good story. Or more precisely, the central question for us should not be, "What personality dynamics explain my behavior?" but rather, "What sort of story am I in?"[25]

The people of our cities are asking the question, "What sort of story am I in?" City ministry enters into the prevailing plotlines of the city and answers this question with the gospel.

What is your city's story? What are the urban idolatries that need to be addressed winsomely by the gospel? And how can that story be rewritten in light of the one-story plotline of the Bible? Asking and answering these questions is key to effective and fruitful ministry in cities. But how does knowing and connecting your city's story with the gospel translate into practical ministry in an urban context? In the final chapter we consider this question, and cast a vision for what God may want to do in your city.

DISCUSSION QUESTIONS

1. What is your city's prevailing story? What do your neighbors tell themselves about the past, present, and future that gives them hope and purpose?

2. Where do your city's story and the story of God's plan of redemption overlap? Can you identify a few potential gospel entry points?
3. Where does your city's story fall short? What are the inherent lies and false promises that your neighbors believe? What is your city promising its citizens that only the gospel can provide?
4. How would you go about winsomely challenging the story of your city in a conversation with an unbelieving friend or coworker?
5. For a moment, imagine that you have fully embraced the broken, unfulfilling story line of your city. In this scenario, what is it about the gospel that strikes you as good news? Identify some of the ways that the gospel provides resolution to your city's story. How does the story of your city find its ultimate completion in the story of the gospel? Why should this be such good news to the inhabitants of your city?

Chapter 6

MINISTRY VISION FOR THE CITY

> Now after these events Paul resolved in the Spirit to pass through Macedonia and Achaia and go to Jerusalem, saying, "After I have been there, I must also see Rome."
>
> **Luke (Acts 19:21)**

How many Christians do you think there were in the year AD 100? How many Christians do you think there were just before Emperor Constantine came on the scene in AD 310? Here is the staggering answer.

AD 100: as few as 25,000 Christians
AD 310: up to 20,000,000 Christians

How did this happen? In two centuries, how did a small band of disciples in AD 33, and then a minority of 25,000 in AD 100, grow from being a small movement to the most potent spiritual force in the Roman Empire?[1]

The answer is cities. The early Christians took the gospel to cities—to major population centers—so that as many people as possible could be transformed by the message of Jesus. Jesus gave his followers a clear mission: "Make disciples of all nations" (Matt. 28:19), and the early Christians carried out this mission largely in cities. Sociologist Rodney Stark states: "Early Christianity was primarily an urban movement. The original meaning of the word pagan (*paganus*) was 'rural person,' or more colloquially 'country hick.' It came to have religious meaning because after Christianity had triumphed in the cities, most of the rural people remained unconverted."[2] From its earliest days Christianity was mainly associated with cities:

> Within twenty years of the crucifixion, Christianity was transformed from a faith based in rural Galilee, to an urban movement reaching far beyond Palestine. . . . All ambitious missionary movements are, or soon become, urban. If the goal is to "make disciples of all nations," missionaries need to go where there are many potential converts, which is precisely what Paul did. His missionary journeys took him to major cities such as Antioch, Corinth, and Athens, with only occasional visits to smaller communities such as Iconium and Laodicea. No mention is made of him preaching in the countryside.[3]

What happened between AD 33 and AD 310 is remarkable. Christians changed the world because of their faithful presence in cities. This is part of our Christian history. We have inherited the legacy of Christians who made their mark in the great cities of antiquity. Our knowledge of the gospel is a result of their faithful stewardship and ministry in cities.

OPPORTUNITY

The early church captivated the entire society by capturing its cities. And two thousand years after the resurrection of Jesus, the greatest opportunity for advancing the gospel of Jesus lies in our cities.

> In 1900, 10 percent of the world's population was urban. By 2005, more than 50 percent of the world's population had become urban. And the trend is accelerating. By 2020 more than 25 cities will have populations in excess of 11 million. By 2050 more than 25 cities will have populations in excess of 16 million. By 2050 four of the top five will be mega-giant cities of 40 million or more (Lagos, Karachi, Mumbai, Dhaka, and Kolkata). And here is a sobering fact: four of those five are likely to be hostile to Christianity.[4]

The future of our world will be profoundly influenced by what happens in the city. "The world is in the throes of a sweeping population shift from the countryside to the city. The global urban population is growing by 65 million annually, equivalent to adding seven new Chicagos a year."[5] Each month, in the developing world there are more than five million people who are migrating and settling in cities.[6]

In the second half of the twentieth century in America, many churches left the city. As a result, Christians lost influence in the culture. But today something new is happening. In North America, South America, Africa, Asia, Europe, and Australia churches are moving back into the city. In their 2011 report on urban growth and the global economy, the McKinsey Global Institute announced how companies need to seize upon this urban growth:

> We live in an urban world. Half of the world's population already lives in cities, generating more than 80 percent of global GDP today. But the urban economic story is even more concentrated than this suggests. Only 600 urban centers, with a fifth of the world's population, generate 60 percent of global GDP. In 2025, we still expect 600 cities to account for about 60 percent of worldwide GDP—but the cities won't be the same. The earth's urban landscape appears to be stable, but its center of gravity is shifting decisively, and at speed. Companies trying to identify the most promising growth opportunities need to be able to map this movement and spot the individual cities where their businesses are most likely to thrive.

What the McKinsey Global Institute recommends for businesses, we recommend for churches. Churches must identify the promising growth opportunities in our cities and figure out how more churches can be planted and more Christians can live, work, worship, and witness in these cities. Yes, churches are needed in the countryside, suburbs, exurbs, villages, and small towns of our world. We are not denying or minimizing that. However, with the radical shift of populations toward cities, the church would be remiss if it did not have a strategic plan to meet the world where it is heading.

VISION

For something significant, sustainable, and supernatural to happen in our cities, we must first have vision. The exiled Israelites flourished in the great city of Babylon, and the city of Babylon flourished because of the Israelites, as a result of vision. Through the prophet Jeremiah, God gave his people a vision to seek the welfare of the city, to pray for the city, and to grow deep and fruitful roots in the city (Jeremiah 29). This countercultural vision set the pace for how God's people would approach life in the city.

Most of us are following some sort of vision for our life or for our church. This is good. But we think God wants us to catch an even bigger vision: a God-sized vision for our city—a picture of the future revealing what our cities could become. But catching such a vision for your city requires a paradigm shift. It means that Christians and churches must exist not for themselves, but for the glory of God and the good of their city.

To gain a God-sized vision we must start with a greater awareness of how we have engaged our cities. Some of us have been living *against* the city, criticizing it rather than trying to help it. Some of us have been living *above* the city, ignoring it and living privatized lives. And some of us need to repent of merely living *in* the city, failing to truly engage and bless it. Our calling is to live *for* the city:

> There are churches that are merely *in* the city. Their heartbeat is to get people in the doors to hear the gospel. That's a good goal. But, unfortunately, that's often where it ends. Such churches create programs for people inside the church walls, and the reach of their ministry only *occasionally* goes outside to the city. The primary focus of these churches is what happens inside the church building. Churches like this are geographically *in* the city, but they aren't effectively engaged with the people and culture of the city.[7]

Have you gravitated more toward living *against, above,* or merely *in* your city?

After honest self-reflection comes prayer. We must ask God to give us his vision for our cities. God cares about our cities far more than we do, so we must seek his vision and heart for them. If we seek God for vision, he will give it. Allow God's Word to shape your prayers. Ask that your church could be a picture of the new city—an alternate city set on a hill that gives light to a dark and broken city (Matt. 5:14–16). Pray that those who are hungry and thirsty, those wandering in desert wastes, and those with fainting souls would cry out for deliverance and be made citizens of a new city (Ps. 107:4–7). Pray for the flourishing of your city. May it be a city marked by justice and equity, where the hungry can dwell and establish themselves through fruitful labor. May it become a flourishing, fruitful, multiplying city that is reminiscent of Eden, which points to the city that is to come (Ps. 107:35–38). Pray that your church can be a spiritual refuge in the city, offering a place of rest and security for sinners, "for the stranger and for the sojourner" (Num. 35:15).

The key here is to dream big, pray big, and ask big. May we never be accused of dreaming too small for our churches and cities; if we're to be accused of something, let it be for having the biggest, loftiest, and most beautiful dreams for our city. Pray toward seeing the number of Christians in your city doubled in the next twenty years. Pray that more and more people would hear and believe the gospel. Pray for more churches to be planted. Pray for a movement of the gospel that is bigger than your church, your programs, and your vision. When you begin praying these big, kingdom prayers, these are the questions that will start to keep you up at night:

What would it look like if a large percentage of my city were to be reached with the gospel?
What would my city feel like if people loved their enemies?
How can the culture and economy of my city make meaningful contributions for the benefit of others around the world?
What are the chief problems, prejudices, and inequalities of my city, and how can Christians participate fruitfully in moving toward a possible solution?

What's most beautiful and good about my city, and how can we
keep building on these strengths for greater flourishing?

What is God's heart for my city?

What if families weren't broken, people weren't killed, nobody
went hungry, the weak weren't abused, the addicted were set
free, the wounded were healed, the warring were at peace, and
lies weren't told in my city?

Is there any reason God could not do in my city what he once did in
a city like Nineveh?

What could my city become over the next thirty years?

What would the apostle Paul say, pray, and do if he were doing
ministry in my city?

What would my city look like if truth, grace, justice, creativity, and
compassion reigned?

Would our city notice if our church no longer existed? Why or
why not?

What if everybody in the city called this place "my city," proudly
identifying with our city and eagerly seeking its well-being?

What if Christians woke up to the reality that we have the best
news in our city, urgent news—good news—that must be
shared?

What if my city worshiped God instead of idols?

We encourage you to wrestle with these questions. Take the
time and the risk to ask these questions prayerfully. Questions can
be powerful. Long ago, in order to stir the hard heart of the prophet
Jonah, God asked him a question: "And should not I pity Nineveh,
that great city, in which there are more than 120,000 persons who do
not know their right hand from their left?" (Jonah 4:11). At the time,
Nineveh was one of the largest, most powerful, and most godless
cities in the world, and yet God cared deeply about it. The answer to
the rhetorical question is, "Yes!" Yes, God should pity and care about
the great city of Nineveh and her 120,000 inhabitants. The same
God who cared about Nineveh, "that great city," cares about your
great city.

The good news for you and your city is that God rules your city,

God cares about your city, God has historically done his great work in cities, and he can change your city. We are not encouraging you to be naive about humanity's fallen condition nor are we suggesting that we engage the city with an optimistic extrapolated triumphalism. The question for us is, will we believe in the power of the gospel to transform human hearts and therefore be motivated to minister courageously with this hope?

KEY ELEMENTS OF CITY MINISTRY

Now that you have a vision for contextualized ministry that relates to your city's story line, what shape will it take? Whatever vision God gives you for your city, we believe that the following four elements must shape our city vision: the gospel, community, balance, and reproduction.

Acts 2:42–47 gives us a picture of the disciples that populated the first urban church. They thrived from the beginning because they had all four of these elements in place:

> They devoted themselves to the apostles' teaching [*gospel*] and the fellowship, to the breaking of bread and the prayers [*community*]. And awe came upon every soul, and many wonders and signs were being done through the apostles. And all who believed were together and had all things in common. And they were selling their possessions and belongings and distributing the proceeds to all, as any had need. And day by day, attending the temple together and breaking bread in their homes, they received their food with glad and generous hearts, praising God and having favor with all the people [*balance*]. And the Lord added to their number day by day those who were being saved [*reproduction*].

As you think about ministry in your city, start by considering these four elemental nonnegotiables. Each is applicable in any context, but the urban context will present unique challenges and opportunities for all four elements. We begin by considering the ultimate nonnegotiable.

The Gospel

The gospel of Jesus Christ must be at the center of all Christian ministry. This is true regardless of context. The gospel does not change when it moves from suburbia to the city. This ought to be a great relief to those seeking to do ministry in our world's cities. Though you will need to do the hard work of contextualization, the gospel itself is "the power of God for salvation" (Rom. 1:16). It does not depend on your savviness, intellect, or ability; it is true and powerful regardless of your qualifications or aptitude. The inverse is also true: no matter how competent or credentialed you may be, your ministry will consistently fall flat if it is not centered on the gospel. For these reasons, it is essential that we get the gospel right before launching into any entailments of gospel ministry in the city.

A Single Gospel. There is one gospel. Though there are many helpful, concise summaries of the gospel, we've found the following statement to get to the heart of the matter:

> We believe that the gospel is the good news of Jesus Christ—God's very wisdom. Utter folly to the world, even though it is the power of God to those who are being saved, this good news is christological, centering on the cross and resurrection: the gospel is not proclaimed if Christ is not proclaimed, and the authentic Christ has not been proclaimed if his death and resurrection are not central (the message is "Christ died for our sins . . . [and] was raised"). This good news is biblical (his death and resurrection are according to the Scriptures), theological and salvific (Christ died for our sins, to reconcile us to God), historical (if the saving events did not happen, our faith is worthless, we are still in our sins, and we are to be pitied more than all others), apostolic (the message was entrusted to and transmitted by the apostles, who were witnesses of these saving events), and intensely personal (where it is received, believed, and held firmly, individual persons are saved).[8]

A faithful ministry is one that is based upon and fascinated by the truth of what God has accomplished in Christ. Notice that the gospel proper is *not* about how we are to respond to God (repentance, faith), or even the necessary implications of the gospel (Christian conduct, life in community, mercy ministries, etc.). The gospel is not advice about how sinners must reach God, but good news about how God has taken action to rescue undeserving sinners. It is a message about what God has done for us, not about what we need to do for him. Knowing the gospel and making these clear distinctions will help you to know just what it is that you are ministering and contextualizing as you seek to do ministry in your city.

A Multifaceted Gospel. Part of the beauty of the gospel is that while it is singular, it is also multifaceted. There is one gospel, but in the Bible it takes a multiplicity of forms. On the most basic level, we can see that the gospel takes different shapes because there are four accounts of the one gospel. Luke articulates the gospel differently than does John; Matthew expresses it differently than Mark. Paul tailored his gospel preaching to his respective audience by drawing on the various facets of the one gospel. He preached to Jews differently than he preached to Gentiles (Gal. 2:7). When preaching to Greeks in Corinth, he presented the gospel in a way that addressed their idol of power (1 Cor. 1:22–25). When preaching to Jews he appealed to their acknowledged authorities (i.e., the Law of Moses and the Prophets, Acts 28:23). Christians who are rightly concerned about maintaining doctrinal orthodoxy need not fear this multifaceted nature of the one gospel, but can celebrate its many forms as evidence of its robustness and sturdiness.[9]

The many forms of the one gospel also offer city Christians multiple points of reference for all of the types of people who are present in an urban context. For aspirational individuals who are seeking self-definition, power, and approval through their work, the gospel offers a selfless Savior whose substitutionary, power-forfeiting self-donation on the cross wins us the approval of God. In turn, our identity is redefined; we are able to wield power through weakness and to work in the freedom of knowing that we have already been approved. For the marginalized person seeking acceptance, community, or wealth, the gospel reveals that one of the essential human problems is a broken relationship with God. Jesus is the substitutionary Son who forfeits the riches of heaven, bears our sin, and becomes willingly unacceptable to the Father, so that we might be accepted, adopted, and made truly rich in Christ. For the explorational individual who seeks pleasure at all costs, Jesus surrenders the pleasures of heaven and voluntarily pays the total cost of our sin by satisfying God's holiness. The result is that we are freed from debt and the prison of our own pleasure seeking. Our truest pleasure and delight are now found in our union with Christ and our citizenship in that future city.

By no means are these the only forms that the gospel takes, but in all forms, Jesus is seen to be the substitutionary Savior who inexplicably gives himself for sinners while assuaging God's wrath and who ultimately fulfills the deepest longings of the human heart. This one gospel in many forms transforms lives, and we are to receive it joyfully by faith. The gospel that we believe must also shape all that we do as we seek to minister in the city.

A Shaping Gospel. There is one unchanging, multifaceted, shaping gospel. When we talk about a "shaping gospel," we mean to say that the implications of the gospel are so far-reaching that every dimension of life and ministry must be shaped by it. There is a difference between believing the gospel as a church and being deeply formed by the gospel:

> It is quite easy to assume that if we understand the gospel accurately and preach it faithfully, our ministry will necessarily be shaped by it—but this is not true. Many churches subscribe to gospel doctrines but do not have a ministry that is shaped by, centered on, and empowered through the gospel. Its implications have not yet worked their way into the fabric of how the church actually does ministry.[10]

City churches must have a comprehensive understanding of the gospel and of its implications. We must not only believe the gospel, we must look like the gospel.

When this is the case, the gospel comes alive on multiple levels: as *doctrinal* news, *personal* news, and *city* news. Doctrine, reading, and preaching become electric when a church rediscovers that the Bible is a book about good news, not good advice. Once the true doctrinal nature of the gospel is continually heralded, people discover that the gospel is personal news that changes everything, most deeply changing one's identity, record, behavior, and future.[11] And this is where most churches stop; they possess a doctrinal and personal perspective on the implications of the gospel, but not a city perspective. To truly impact our cities, city churches must show that the gospel announces good news not only to individuals, but also to the city. As we argued in chapter 3, God has a plan to end injustice and suffering in our cities, to bring healing and restoration to the world (Rom. 8:21; Col. 1:20), through a heaven-sent city. In that city, forgiven people will eternally dwell in perfect unity, worshiping the one true God. Without this layer of the implications of the gospel, our city ministry could become inward and individualistic, completely missing the complexity of brokenness in our world and God's heart to renew all things through the sacrificial power of his Son.

What does a gospel-shaped church look like? Let's address how a robust understanding of the shaping influence of the gospel might affect the way that a church worships. Much of what passes for Christian worship in our cities is mere moralism or cheap grace. Moralism leads to dour and somber worship, which may be long on dignity, but short on joy. Non-Christians will be immediately turned off. Cheap grace, a shallow understanding of acceptance without a sense of God's holiness, can lead to sentimental, powerless, casual worship, which again offers no hope to unbelievers in the city.[12] It's also possible to encounter worship that omits both God's love and holiness, leading to a worship service that feels like a committee meeting. But the gospel leads a people to see that God is both transcendent and immanent.

His immanence makes his transcendence comforting, while his transcendence makes his immanence amazing. The gospel leads a church to experience both awe and intimacy in worship, for, because of the substitutionary work of Jesus, God is now our Father.

A worship service that is shaped by this gospel is much different than merely mentioning Jesus or reciting a sentence of doctrine. Instead, Jesus is experienced as the center and object of our worship. As this worship is made accessible to the people of the city, lives are changed. In this way, we must shape the entirety of our ministry in the city around constant communication of the good news, which is multilayered. Our experience is that many people in the city are hungry to hear good news and ready to leave behind idolatry and belief systems that have left them empty and disillusioned. There is no better place for this to happen than in a gospel-shaped church where the unchanging gospel is contextually communicated in all its beautiful facets.

Is this gospel deeply shaping the life of your church and being communicated to your city?

Community

People don't move to Silicon Valley for relationships; they move for work. People don't move to Boston for community; they move to receive an education for professional advancement. And so it goes in most cities of our world—people are chasing their dreams in our cities, but doing so alone. Scratch beneath the surface of most city dwellers, people who have left behind traditional ties of family, place, and belonging, and you'll discover loneliness. It's ironic that in the city, where people live closest to one another, people can be the loneliest.

The gospel creates a community that is the solution to the loneliness in our cities. Jesus told his disciples that they were to be "a city set on a hill" that cannot be hidden (Matt. 5:14). Jesus called his people to be a city within a city, a community of people who model to the city what human relationships are supposed to look like. As we observed in Acts 2, the first city church was one that studied, fellowshipped, ate, prayed, shared, sacrificed, and enjoyed life with one another. The result was that they had "favor with all people," and "the Lord added to their number day by day " (v. 47). The gospel created a community that was not only attractive to the watching world, but also appealing to large numbers of people who were compelled to join.

Unfortunately, our churches don't often model this community. It's been said that church small groups mainly "provide occasions for individuals to focus on themselves in the presence of others."[13] To do meaningful ministry in our cities, we must enjoy and model the community that God created us for:

> Through the gospel we gain a new community, a new family of deep friendship with brothers and sisters in Christ who come from all walks of life. We grow in Christ and put his love on display as we open up our lives to participate in community that's built upon grace. The church is not a meeting you attend, it is a network of relationships you belong to—relationships that share a common confession and mission. As we do life together in community, with God's Word at the center, disciples are made. Jesus changes us and uses us. He shrinks our pride and surfaces our gifts. We come to see that all people stand on equal ground at the foot of the cross, giving us a freeing humility that welcomes the messy and glorious work of church community. Our model for community is our Triune God— Father, Son, and Spirit who have eternally enjoyed loving, servant-hearted community.[14]

One of the greatest apologetics for the gospel in our cities is community. It was Jesus who said, "By this all people will know that you are my disciples, if you have love for one another" (John 13:35). The place where we experience the greatest joy in life is also the place where we experience the greatest pain: relationships. The people of our cities are accustomed to seeing relationships fail; they are not accustomed to seeing a community that covenants to love one another, love outsiders, and follow a Savior who died for his enemies. Unfortunately, our cities often see churches that model transactional community—relationships that last so long as someone is benefiting from it. The church has often modeled moralistic or liberal community, not biblical community. Moralism makes relationships hinge on performance, where navigating conflict in community becomes a never-ending blame game or an attempt at self-justification. Liberalism reduces relationships and love to a negotiated partnership for mutual benefit, to arrangements that last so long as both parties are happy and having their needs met. But the gospel creates a community where sacrifice, service, and commitment are the norm. A gospel-shaped community is one in which we love one another enough to speak the truth in love, and are committed to stay with one another even when it doesn't benefit us. Gospel community is a covenantal relationship between a king and his servants, not a commercial one between a vendor and a consumer.

Though people often move to cities for reasons other than community, cities are a strong testament to the community for which we were created. According to Glaeser, "The enduring strength of cities reflects the profoundly social nature of humanity. Our ability to connect with one another is the defining characteristic of our species."[15] The problem is that our cities (and many churches) try to achieve community by putting community at the center. Scripture calls us to find community by putting God at the center. As churches focus on the triune God who suffered and sacrificed to bring us into community with himself, we can experience and model something that our cities rarely see: the reconciling grace of God at work in human relationships.

> Christians in community are never to give up on one another. We must never tire of forgiving (and/or repenting) and seeking to repair our relationships. . . . God always holds you responsible to reach out to repair a broken relationship. A Christian is responsible to begin the process of reconciliation, regardless of how the distance or alienation began.[16]

Our dense and diverse cities must see in our churches a picture of what life will look like in the new city. In the microcontext of our "city on a hill" communities, we must foreshadow the sweeping restoration and renewal that God has promised to bring about in the macrocontext of the future city. According to Acts 2, lives were changed and cities were blessed not only by hearing the gospel message proclaimed, but also by watching the gospel message at work in a community of disciples who loved one another and loved the people of their city. We pray that the shaping influence of the gospel would transform our communities into attractive, compelling witnesses of the reconciling grace of God.

Is this the kind of community your church models to your city?

Balance

Cities are deeply complex places. Clustered density and connective diversity lead to the amplification of both ingenuity and idolatry, which results in cities having an endless number of possibilities and problems. Simply put, there are any number of different things that a ministry in the city might do. The question is, what are the things that a city ministry *must* do? As we've seen, a city ministry must get the gospel right. This must also happen in a community that is radically shaped by the gospel. But on what will this gospel-shaped urban community expend its resources? What should city churches spend their time doing? For what should we be known?

If you walk around your city on a Sunday morning, you will likely find churches that are known for any number of things. Each will have a unique emphasis—things it does well and other things that it does poorly. One church is known for its strong emphasis on gospel proclamation, but it lacks a gospel-driven concern for the poor. Another church has a heavy emphasis on community, but because it's somewhat insular, it fails to equip its people for mission. A historic church has a remarkable ministry to the poor and marginalized, but there is little in its preaching to distinguish it as a Christian church. The point of these caricatures is not to insult various ministry models. Instead, we simply hope to show that churches have strengths and weaknesses, and unless we are intentional about working toward a balanced ministry, our churches will inevitably be lopsided. What is essential is that our churches contextualize and preach the gospel in such a way that the city's story is retold, its needs are addressed, and its flourishing is encouraged. No one has brought more clarity to this subject than Tim Keller. In *Center Church*, he suggests that city churches must seek an integrative balance between four "ministry fronts." We'll briefly survey them here.

Evangelistic Worship. City churches must connect people to God through the gospel. They can best do this through gospel-centered, evangelistic, corporate worship. Clear, contextualized worship services that place the good news of Jesus Christ at their center are the bread and butter of the faithful city church. Our speech, prayers, songs, liturgy, and preaching must all be shaped by the good news of what God has done for his people in redemptive history.

This worship is evangelistic in the sense that city churches must always communicate the gospel to both Christians and non-Christians. City churches live with the three realities of clustered density, hypermobility, and cosmopolitan skepticism. This means that significant numbers of new people will enter your church each and every Sunday, and that many of them will be confessing skeptics who are somewhat open to hearing the claims of the gospel. This being the case, we must strive to present the gospel in such a way that both Christians and non-Christians will understand. We are not suggesting a seeker-sensitive model, but a skeptic-intelligible model. Accordingly, our speech should be winsome and clear, not unnecessarily spiritualized. Our tone should be respectful and humble, not haughty or antagonistic. We should avoid insider jargon, or carrying on as if unbelievers are not present. In all of this, the goal is to offer a comprehensible, challenging, compelling invitation to life with God through the gospel.

Your city is a center of worship where people predominantly worship false idols. Sunday worship is the primary venue in which you publicly display what it looks like to worship the one true God rightly. As such, it is also the context in which you address your city's values, hopes, and fears with the gospel, showing Christ to be the fulfiller and resolver of all the tensions present in your city's story. In this way, urban idolatries are unmasked, and the one true God is seen to be the only hope for the inhabitants of your city.

Community and Discipleship. Although we have already spent a significant amount of time talking about community, it is hard to overestimate how essential an organic, vibrant gospel community is for ministry in the city. Apart from preaching, it is the church's greatest asset in displaying the good news of the gospel. Cities are filled with isolated, overworked, out-of-balance people. In our churches, we have the opportunity to show how the gospel overcomes all barriers to eradicate isolation. It is our task to demonstrate that true rest and stability are found in Christ alone. The church is called to be a "city on a hill" that people look at and say, "I want to live in that city . . . forever." As such, every aspect of our community and discipleship ought to be affected by the reality that we have been entrusted with the responsibility to lead and equip the citizens of God's city.[17] Though we will always fall short of that ideal, our faltering attempts at foreshadowing the new city will give us the opportunity to invite people to transfer their primary citizenship to "the city of the living God, the heavenly Jerusalem" (Heb. 12:22).

Social Justice and Mercy. When we're given a picture of the future city, here's what we find has happened to all of the fallenness and brokenness that now surround us: "He will wipe away every tear from their eyes, and death shall be no more, neither shall there be mourning, nor crying, nor pain anymore" (Rev. 21:4). The picture is one of weary pilgrims who have at last found their ultimate rest: "To the thirsty I will give from the spring of the water of life without payment" (Rev. 21:6). Sin and its effects have been obliterated and removed. All tribes and nations live in absolute harmony (Rev. 5:9). God has finished his ultimate renewal project.

When we look at Acts, it appears that the early church modeled this kind of renewed community to their cities. They "were selling their possessions and belongings and distributing the proceeds to all, as any had need" (2:45). This was at least part of what gave them "favor with all the people," and was likely a compelling reason why many were "added to their number day by day" (2:47). Though we are not advocating for Christians to sell all of their belongings, we are calling for a recovery of the radical, sacrificial generosity that is a necessary result of the gospel. How do you explain the rapid growth of the church in the first few centuries? Sociologist Rodney Stark observes:

> To cities filled with the homeless and impoverished, Christianity offered charity as well as hope. To cities filled with newcomers and strangers, Christianity offered an immediate basis for attachments. To cities filled with widows and orphans, Christianity provided a new and expanded sense of family. To cities torn by violent ethnic strife, Christianity offered a new basis for social solidarity. And to cities faced with epidemics, fires, and earthquakes, Christianity offered effective nursing services. . . . When Christianity [appeared], its superior capacity for meeting these chronic problems soon became evident and played a major role in its ultimate triumph . . . [for what Christians] brought was not simply an urban movement, but a new culture.[18]

The gospel enables and encourages Christians to care not only for their own—we must *at least* do that—but also for the poor, marginalized, and alienated. The generosity at work in the institutional church ought to overflow into the city by way of the organic church,[19] as individual Christians catch a vision of God's ultimate urban renewal plan. And one of the primary ways that Christians do justice and show mercy is through the integration of faith and work.

Integration of Faith and Work. The importance of work is something the world has never neglected, but which the church seems to have forgotten. While the world is constantly talking about work, the church speaks little about what people predominantly do each week in their waking hours. Outside of the city, it's more common for people to equate being a faithful Christian with frequently showing up at church activities. Inside of the city, it's more common for people to ask how they can be faithful Christians outside of the church, particularly in relation to their work.

City people often do not have significant private lives since they are consumed by work. So the church must equip people to pursue their vocations in a distinctively Christian manner. The diverse vocations at play in our churches and cities—engineers, teachers, baristas, entrepreneurs, stay-at-home moms, financial planners, day laborers, architects, students, small business owners, CEOs, nurses, real estate agents, nonprofit leaders, etc.—all share a common purpose: to help others flourish. This is the summation of the Bible's teaching on work—our work is meant to help others flourish. Yet each of these vocations carries unique challenges, opportunities, and temptations. City churches will not significantly impact their city unless they equip their people to carry out their diverse vocations in a manner deeply integrated with their faith.

Sadly, "traditional evangelical ministries tend to give believers relatively little help in understanding how they can maintain their Christian practice outside the walls of the church while still participating in the world of the arts and theatre, business and finance, scholarship and learning, and government and public policy."[20]

In contrast, a thick understanding of how the gospel affects all of life leads to a rich, full understanding of the value and importance of work. Believing this, a gospel-shaped city church seeks opportunities to unleash people to carry out their distinctive vocations in the city. City Christians look to love their neighbor with whatever is needed—conversion or a cup of cold water, salvation or a new sewer system, Bibles or blueprints. Of course, we are not saying that our vocational work *is* the gospel or that it is more important than Christian conversion or worship, but we are saying that true Christianity will display its entailments and implications to every dimension of human life.

Indeed, "we Christians are the only people who can truly discuss the salvation of souls and the rebuilding of city sewer systems in the same sentence."[21] The best thing we can do in our churches is equip and unleash our people to minister to the city through their vocations.

The gospel can free the people in your city from overworking to placate their idols. The gospel can provide the deep rest for which every person in your city longs. The gospel undergirds and spurs on human creativity that flourishes humanity. The gospel liberates us from the slavery of self-interest and enables us to work for the benefit of others. Applying the gospel to work in this way is one of the greatest gifts that the church can give its people. In turn, one of the good gifts that a church can give to its city is a significant number of gospel-driven individuals in every field and discipline.[22]

Summary. As Keller has noted, "Engaging on all of these fronts is required by the nature of the gospel. The experience of gospel grace inspires evangelism as well as intimate, glorious worship of the God who saved us. It creates the new transparency and openness that make deep fellowship possible. The grace orientation of the gospel humbles us and gives us a new passion for justice. And the nature of the gospel helps us discern idolatry in ourselves and in our culture that distorts the way we do our work and live our lives in society."[23]

Is your church publicly, intelligibly displaying what it looks like to worship the one true God? Does your community present a compelling picture of what life will look like in the future city? Has the gospel transformed the way that the people in your church respond to issues of mercy and social justice? Do the people of your church understand the vocational calling they have in your city?

Reproduction

Twenty-five years ago, Peter Wagner famously declared, "Planting new churches is the most effective evangelistic methodology known under heaven."[24] We agree with Wagner. The Great Commission was instinctively carried out in the first century by disciples who planted new churches in new cities. Church planting was the normal mode of operation for the early church, and it should be the normal mode of operation for all who want to reach our rapidly growing cities. The gospel doesn't only create well-balanced communities; it spawns reproducing communities. Just as healthy families reproduce, healthy disciples and healthy churches reproduce.

As we write, church growth is desperately lagging behind the exponential population growth in our major cities. The only way to impact these growing populations is for churches to set a course of regular reproduction—starting, sending out, and supporting new church plants throughout the city. Both of our churches are committed to larger networks that have set an aggressive course and commitment to church planting. Stephen belongs to Redeemer City to City, a network with a mission that goes beyond church planting: "Our mission is to help leaders build gospel movements in cities."[25] Justin belongs to the Acts 29 Network, which in its short tenure has helped plant over four hundred churches in the United States and throughout the world, with a heavy focus on city church planting.[26]

As the Redeemer City to City mission statement implies, it takes a movement to reach a city. The beating heart of multiplication is church planting. But for city church planting to truly make a dent in our cities, churches must work together to participate in a larger movement. To reach a large portion of a city with the gospel, many different types of churches are needed. Some segments of the population will be best reached by a nondenominational church, others by a Presbyterian church; some by a very large church, others by a small church; some by a highly programmed church, others by a low program church. Additional gospel-proclaiming churches in our city are not our competition, they are our friends, helping advance the mission that Jesus gave us. We should pray for gospel growth and city growth, not only for church growth. Both of our church planting networks break down into smaller regional networks that work together with other church-planting ministries in the city to help multiply churches.[27] We sense that the future lies in such partnerships: diverse city churches and city networks partnering together to train, fund, start, and support a great diversity of new churches that uniquely carry out these four elements of city ministry that we've been outlining.

To pursue multiplication in this way, we must be Christians who are deeply concerned about the kingdom of God just as we are about our own particular church. This comes from having a city vision, not merely a vision for our own church. Our objective isn't to use the city to build great churches, but to start and lead churches in order to seek a great and flourishing city.

Is your church intentionally pursuing reproduction?

Patience, Hard Work, and Prayer

Lest there be any misunderstanding, we want to clearly state that nothing we have written and urged in this book is easy to do. It is all very difficult. The vision we are casting and ministry we are recommending for our cities demand patience, hard work, and prayer. There are no shortcuts.

It takes time for people to change. It takes even longer for cities to change. The ministry we are calling for mainly involves a lot of hard work and prayer. This is why you must have God-given vision to pursue the welfare of your city; it's the vision that will sustain you when you grow weary. To truly impact our cities we must live long term in our cities, growing deep roots and laboring toward a better future for our cities. Our cities are used to having people who come into the city to use it, and then leave it. What our cities are not accustomed to are people who come to the city to serve, to stay, and to love it.

Old-fashioned patience, hard work, and prayer must be the rebar that runs through all of our contextualized gospel ministry in the city. Both of us have experienced (and are experiencing) that we are in way over our heads as we seek to lead our churches in our cities. Our prayer lives are now far more dynamic than when we did ministry that felt more manageable. We like it this way, constantly feeling the need to talk to God and ask for his help. And God gives this help. Cities are his idea. God cares about the welfare of our cities more than we do. And perhaps one day, after a lot of patience and prayer, our cities will reach a tipping point, and our city visions will begin to be realized:

> How likely is it that an urban gospel movement could grow so strong that it reaches a city-changing "tipping point" at which time the gospel begins having a visible impact on the city-life and culture produced there? We know this can happen through God's grace. The history books give us examples. However, only the very rare Christian leaders, like John Wesley, will live to see the movement they have begun grow to such a level of effectiveness. So urban ministers should make this their goal, and give their whole lives to it, but not expect to see it in their own lifetimes. That's the right balance between expectation and patience that we need to strike, if we are going to see our cities loved and reached for Christ.[28]

This is what gets us out of bed in the morning, giving our lives to something we dream of seeing in our cities. God has done it before, so we know he can do it again. The phrase "soul of the city" comes from an ancient letter describing Christians and the impact they made in the city. In AD 140 the *Letter to Diognetus* was written, a letter to a government official arguing that Christians were not a threat to the city, but that Christians are the heart and soul of a city. Though too long to quote in full, the heart of the letter states the stunning result of Christians simply living as Christians in a fallen world:

> Christians are indistinguishable from other men either by nationality, language or customs. They do not inhabit separate cities of their own, or speak a strange dialect, or follow some outlandish way of life. . . . With regard to dress, food and manner of life in general, they follow the customs of whatever city they happen to be living in, whether it is Greek or foreign. And yet there is something extraordinary about their lives. They live in their own countries as though

they were only passing through. They play their full role as citizens, but labor under all the disabilities of aliens. . . . Like others, they marry and have children, but they do not expose them. They share their meals, but not their wives. . . .

They pass their days upon earth, but they are citizens of heaven. Obedient to the laws, they yet live on a level that transcends the law. Christians love all men, but all men persecute them. Condemned because they are not understood, they are put to death, but raised to life again. They live in poverty, but enrich many; they are totally destitute, but possess an abundance of everything. They suffer dishonor, but that is their glory. They are defamed, but vindicated. A blessing is their answer to abuse, deference their response to insult. . . .

To speak in general terms, we may say that the Christian is to the world what the soul is to the body. As the soul is present in every part of the body, while remaining distinct from it, so Christians are found in all the cities of the world, but cannot be identified with the world. As the visible body contains the invisible soul, so Christians are seen living in the world, but their religious life remains unseen. . . . It is by the soul, enclosed within the body, that the body is held together, and similarly, it is by the Christians, detained in the world as in a prison, that the world is held together. The soul, though immortal, has a mortal dwelling place; and Christians also live for a time amidst perishable things, while awaiting the freedom from change and decay that will be theirs in heaven.[29]

We see no reason why this heritage cannot be recovered in our day. Once again Christians can become the soul of the city, living lives of supernatural dependence on the grace of God and sacrificial service to our broken cities. Though we don't know exactly what is in store for the cities we love, we do know what is in store for the city that we will always call home.

THE CITY TO COME

Jesus has promised to build two things: his church (Matt. 16:18) and a new city (Revelation 21). What Jesus is currently doing with his church, his city within a city, will one day culminate in the city to come—the joining of heaven and earth in an eternal city where the redeemed will finally see God face to face and discover that everything sad, fallen, or twisted has become untrue. The work we do in our cities today, no matter how fruitful or unfruitful, will not be wasted. All things will be redeemed by the God who suffered to save us and give us an eternal city in which to dwell. It is a city where there will be no more tears, pain, death, darkness, or sadness, but only the perfect presence of our triune God and his people.

About sixteen hundred years ago Saint Augustine finished writing his masterpiece, the voluminous *City of God*. In the last chapter Augustine wrote, nearly as eloquently as the apostle John wrote in Revelation, of the city that is to come:

> Who can measure the happiness of heaven, where no evil at all can touch us, no good will be out of reach; where life is to be one long laud extolling God. . . . God will be the source of every satisfaction, more than any heart can rightly crave, more than life and health, food and wealth, glory and honor, peace and every good—so that God, as St. Paul said, "may be all in all" (1 Cor. 15:28). He will be the consummation of all our desiring—the object of our unending vision, of our unlessening love, of our unwearying praise . . . in the everlasting City, there will remain in each and all of us an inalienable freedom of the will, emancipating us from every evil and filling us with every good, rejoicing in the inexhaustible beatitude of everlasting happiness, unclouded by the memory of any sin or of sanction suffered, yet with no forgetfulness of our redemption nor any loss of gratitude for our Redeemer. . . . And, surely, in all that City, nothing will be lovelier than this song in praise of the grace of Christ by whose Blood all there were saved. . . . On that day we shall rest and see, see and love, love and praise—for this is to be the end without the end of all our living, that Kingdom without end, the real goal of our present life.[30]

Friends, this is our future. Until then, we have a lot of work to do. Cities matter. Let's get to it.[31]

DISCUSSION QUESTIONS

1. When you consider the holistic life of your city, what are some of the unique opportunities for gospel witness that you may have previously overlooked?

2. Try to describe God's vision for your city. What would it look like to develop a vision for your city that is out of the reach of any individual, church, or network?

3. Take another look at this chapter's section on the gospel. Are you utterly convinced that the gospel must be at the center of all that you do? What are some ways that you can continue to drive this point home in your own life and in the life of your community?

4. What is the significance of the witness of a community in a city? How can the gathered church communicate the gospel in ways that individuals cannot? How would you describe your church's public witness to the city? Does the significance of community witness underscore the importance of church planting?

5. How can fixing our eyes on the city that is to come encourage us in our gospel ministry in our cities? How does the security of our future "urban" home affect the way that we live and minister in the present?

RECOMMENDED READING

Though we may not agree with every theory or opinion put forward in these books, we have found them to be helpful guides in thinking about urbanization and the importance of doing gospel ministry in the cities of our world. "Essential" reads are marked with an (*).

City Past, Present, and Future

Richard Florida. *Who's Your City? How the Creative Economy Is Making Where You Live the Most Important Decision of Your Life.* New York: Basic, 2009.

*Edward Glaeser. *Triumph of the City: How Our Greatest Invention Makes Us Richer, Smarter, Greener, Healthier, and Happier.* New York: Penguin, 2011.

Jane Jacobs. *The Death and Life of Great American Cities.* New York: Modern Library, 1993.

Joel Kotkin. *The City: A Global History.* New York: Modern Library, 2006.

Lewis Mumford. *The City in History: Its Origins, Its Transformations, and Its Prospects.* New York: Harcourt, 1961.

City Vision

Collin Hansen and John Woodbridge. *A God-Sized Vision: Revival Stories That Stretch and Stir.* Grand Rapids, MI: Zondervan, 2010.

*Rodney Stark. *The Cities of God: The Real Story of How Christianity Became an Urban Movement and Conquered Rome.* New York: HarperCollins, 2006.

_____. *The Rise of Christianity: How the Obscure, Marginal Jesus Movement Became the Dominant Religious Force in the Western World in a Few Centuries.* HarperSanFrancisco, 1997.

City Ministry

Augustine. *City of God; An Abridged Version.* Edited by Vernon J. Bourke. New York: Doubleday, 1958.

D. A. Carson and Timothy Keller, eds. *The Gospel as Center: Renewing Our Faith and Reforming Our Ministry Practices.* Wheaton, IL: Crossway, 2012.

Matt Carter and Darrin Patrick. *For the City: Proclaiming and Living Out the Gospel.* Grand Rapids, MI: Zondervan, 2010.

*Harvie M. Conn and Manuel Ortiz. *Urban Ministry: The Kingdom, the City & the People of God.* Downers Grove, IL: IVP Academic, 2001.

James Davidson Hunter. *To Change the World: The Irony, Tragedy, and Possibility of Christianity in a Late Modern World.* New York: Oxford University Press, 2010.

*Timothy J. Keller. *Center Church: Doing Balanced, Gospel-Centered Ministry in Your City.* Grand Rapids, MI: Zondervan, 2012.

_____. *Generous Justice: How God's Grace Makes Us Just.* New York: Dutton, 2010.

Amy L. Sherman. *Kingdom Calling: Vocational Stewardship for the Common Good.* Downers Grove, IL: InterVarsity, 2011.

NOTES

Foreword

1. Jim Clifton, *The Coming Jobs War: What Every Leader Must Know About the Future of Job Creation* (New York: Gallup Press, 2011), 63.
2. Ian Wylie, "Knowledge Is Power," *The Guardian* (September 30, 2008).
3. *The Guardian*, "Rise of the Megacities," http://image.guardian.co.uk/sys-images/Observer/Pix/pictures/2012/01/21/urban2.jpg/.
4. Parag Khanna, "Beyond City Limits," FP, http://www.foreignpolicy.com/articles/2010/08/16/beyond_city_limits/.
5. Albert Mohler, "From Megacity to 'Metacity'—The Shape of the Future," AlbertMohler.com, http://www.albertmohler.com/2010/04/22/from-megacity-to-metacity-the-shape-of-the-future/.

Introduction

1. For our working definition of "the gospel," please see our discussion in chapter 6, 130–34.
2. While some might immediately dismiss these statements as a caricature, research suggests, unfortunately, that there is a quantifiable anti-urban bias at play within American evangelicalism. "Historical sources, coupled with the data that is available, suggests that evangelicalism may amplify and exacerbate a more generally American anti-urban bias." Mark T. Mulder and James K. A. Smith, "Subdivided by Faith? An Historical Account of Evangelicals and the City," *Christian Scholars Review* 38, no. 4 (2009): 433. We hope that this will clarify why we have written *Why Cities Matter*. Evidence shows that the world is rapidly becoming more urban, *and* that there have been evangelicals in our recent past who embody an anti-urban bias. We argue for the importance of cities not because it is sexy or trendy, but because the wonderfully good news of the gospel demands that our mission not be haphazard or arbitrary. Rather, Christian mission ought to be strategic. Yes, people are people wherever you find them, and they are all equally in need of the gospel. But the fact is that we will increasingly find more and more people in our world's cities. In no way does this suggest that people in cities are more valuable or "gospel-worthy" than people in the suburbs. Nor does this suggest that churches and ministries in cities are more important or valuable than churches in suburban and rural areas. On the contrary, we need gospel-preaching churches everywhere. *Why Cities Matter* was written be-

cause—despite the headlines about hip urban areas—urban areas need faithful, gospel-preaching churches more than they ever have before.

Chapter 1: The Importance of Cities

1. Doug Saunders, *Arrival City: How the Largest Migration in History Is Reshaping Our World* (New York: Pantheon, 2010), 1.
2. *U.S. News & World Report*, "National University Rankings," http://col leges.usnews.rankingsandreviews.com/best-colleges/rankings/nation al-universities/ (accessed January 11, 2012); Massachusetts Institute of Technology, "MIT Facts: Faculty and Staff," http://web.mit.edu/facts/fac ulty.html/ (accessed January 11, 2012).
3. *U.S. News & World Report*, "Best Hospitals 2011–12: the Honor Roll," http:// health.usnews.com/health-news/best-hospitals/articles/2011/07/18 /best-hospitals-2011-12-the-honor-roll/ (accessed January 11, 2012).
4. City of Boston, "Boston Common," http://www.cityofboston.gov/free domtrail/ bostoncommon.asp (accessed January 11, 2012).
5. A two-mile radius placed at 42.351139/-71.064935 encompasses much of what has come to be thought of as center-city Boston, as well as a significant portion of its sister city, Cambridge.
6. As of the 2010 census, Boston proper has a population of about 618,000. See Boston Redevelopment Authority, "Boston: 2010 Census Population," bostonredevelopmentauthority.org, http://www.bostonredevelopmentau thority.org/PDF/ResearchPublications//Boston.pdf/ (accessed February 6, 2012).
7. Edward Glaeser, *Triumph of the City: How Our Greatest Invention Makes Us Richer, Smarter, Greener, Healthier, and Happier* (New York: Penguin, 2011), 1.
8. Harvie M. Conn and Manuel Ortiz, *Urban Ministry: The Kingdom, the City & the People of God* (Downers Grove, IL: IVP Academic, 2001), 34–35.
9. Joel Kotkin, *The City: A Global History* (New York: Modern Library, 2006), ixx.
10. Lewis Mumford, *The City in History: Its Origins, Its Transformations, and Its Prospects* (New York: Harcourt, 1961), 74–75. See also Kotkin, *The City*, 33.
11. Kotkin, *The City*, 3–5.
12. For this section we broadly follow Harvie Conn's four-wave approach to urban history. See Conn and Ortiz, *Urban Ministry*, 35–79.
13. Michael Grant, *From Alexandra to Cleopatra: The Hellenistic World* (New York: Scribner's, 1982), as quoted in Kotkin, *The City*, 25.
14. Cities suffered to the extent that they ceased to be generative centers. This often happened when a formerly thriving city was taken over for a personal fief by a secular or religious authority. See Conn and Ortiz,

Urban Ministry, 164. Also, Richard G. Fox, *Urban Anthropology: Cities in Their Cultural Settings* (Englewood Cliffs, NJ: Prentice Hall, 1977).

15. Craig G. Bartholomew, *Where Mortals Dwell: A Christian View of Place Today* (Grand Rapids, MI: Baker Academic, 2011), 253; Conn and Ortiz, *Urban Ministry*, 41.

16. Bartholomew, *Where Mortals Dwell*, 253.

17. Kotkin, *The City*, 75.

18. Conn and Ortiz, *Urban Ministry*, 42.

19. Alister McGrath offers additional perspective: "The Reformation may be regarded as a necessary, and perhaps overdue, attempt to relate the gospel to the new world of the cities, in which the laity were increasingly playing a dominant role—precisely the same social, personal, and existential concerns that believers have today." *Spirituality in an Age of Change: Rediscovering the Spirit of the Reformers* (Grand Rapids, MI: Zondervan, 1994), 23.

20. Conn and Ortiz, *Urban Ministry*, 50–52.

21. Kotkin, *The City*, 98.

22. Population Reference Bureau, "Human Population: Urbanization," http://www.prb.org/Educators/TeachersGuides/HumanPopulation/Urbanization.aspx/ (accessed February 12, 2012); Population Reference Bureau, "2011 World Population Data Sheet: The World at 7 Billion," http://www.prb.org/pdf11/2011population-data-sheet_eng.pdf/ (accessed February 12, 2012).

23. Population Reference Bureau, "Human Population: Urbanization" (accessed February 12, 2012).

24. Robert X. Cringley, "The Five Rules of Prognostication," *Forbes*, http://www.forbes.com/asap/1998/1130/036.html/ (accessed February 12, 2012).

25. United Nations, Department of Economic and Social Affairs, Population Division, "World Urbanization Prospects, the 2011 Revision," http://esa.un.org/unpd/wup/index.htm/ (accessed April 9, 2012).

26. United Nations, Department of Economic and Social Affairs, Population Division, "Urban and Rural Areas, 2009," http://esa.un.org/unpd/wup/Documents/WUP2009_Wallchart_Urban-Rural_Final.pdf/ (accessed February 13, 2012).

27. United Nations, Department of Economic and Social Affairs, Population Division, "World Urbanization Prospects, 2009: Highlights," http://esa.un.org/unpd/wup/Documents/WUP2009_Highlights_Final.pdf/ (accessed February 13, 2012).

28. United Nations, "Urban and Rural Areas, 2009." These numbers are based on the UN's estimates for Asia as a whole. We have excluded the population of Japan as it is considered an already-developed country by the UN.

29. *Bloomberg News*, "China's Urban Population Exceeds Countryside for First Time," http://www.bloomberg.com/news/2012-01-17/china-urban -population-exceeds-rural.html/ (accessed January 19, 2012).

30. Glaeser, *Triumph of the City*, 7.

31. Ibid., 6. The whole definition includes "people and companies." We have chosen to omit "companies" in our reference for two reasons: (1) To universalize Glaeser's definition, making it applicable to places around the globe and throughout history where "companies" are not essential to the existence of a city; and (2) Glaeser is an economist whose understanding of the city is broadly shaped by commercial structures. We will suggest that additional structures may be just as important to the life of cities as the economic piece.

32. Ibid., 9.

33. We've replaced Kotkin's "busy" with "social." *The City*, xix.

34. We use the word "power" here in its neutral sense. Though many speak of power in wholly negative terms, the structures that we associate with power (economy, politics, defense, etc.) are neutral in and of themselves. Power itself is neutral. The way power is wielded is the basis upon which it must be judged.

35. Conn and Ortiz, *Urban Ministry*, 35.

36. An interesting piece on the role of migration and immigration in the global phenomenon of urbanization is Doug Sanders's *Arrival City*.

37. Richard Florida, *Who's Your City? How the Creative Economy Is Making Where You Live the Most Important Decision of Your Life* (New York: Basic, 2009), 9.

38. Ibid., 48.

39. Richard Florida, "The 25 Most Economically Powerful Cities in the World," The Atlantic Cities, http://www.theatlanticcities.com/jobs-and -economy/2011/09/25-most-economically-powerful-cities-world/109 /#slide2/ (accessed January 26, 2012).

40. An observation made by Glaeser, *Triumph of the City*, 70. For Glaeser, the moral question is, what are cities doing to ensure that the path out of poverty is accessible to all (better transit, public schools, etc.)? In a conversation with Stephen, sociologist Sassia Sasken, author of *The Global City: New York, London, Tokyo* (Princeton, NJ: Princeton University Press, 2001), put forward the view that cities are often exploited by systems that make social inequality. So, while cities often provide solutions to the problems that they create, there may be times when the city itself is exploited in such a way that cycles of poverty and injustice are perpetuated.

41. John Reader, *Cities* (New York: Atlantic Monthly Press, 2004), 306.

42. Our working definition of culture is that of Lesslie Newbigin: culture is "the sum total of ways of living built up by a human community and transmitted from one generation to another." *The Other Side of 1984: Questions for the Churches* (Geneva: World Council of Churches, 1983), 5. Andy Crouch provides another helpful, brief definition: "Culture is what we make of the world." *Culture Making: Recovering Our Creative Calling* (Downers Grove, IL: InterVarsity, 2008), 23.

43. With the rise of the postindustrial city, it would seem that we may be overstating the case on this last point, but between the concentration of tech in global cities, and the significant number of cities that are still centered on industry, we feel confident that between design and production, all modern technology bears the fingerprint of the city.

44. Joel Kotkin, "Why America's Young and Restless Will Abandon Cities for Suburbs," *Forbes*, http://www.forbes.com/sites/joelkotkin/2011/07/20/why-americas-young-and-restless-will-abandon-cities-for-suburbs/ (accessed December 15, 2011).

45. Timothy J. Keller, *Center Church: Doing Balanced, Gospel-Centered Ministry in Your City* (Grand Rapids, MI: Zondervan, 2012), 149.

46. Mumford, *The City in History*, 10.

47. Ibid., 9.

48. Jonathan Merritt, "What Skyscrapers Tell Us . . . About Us," Q: Ideas for the Common Good, http://www.qideas.org/blog/what-skyscrapers-tell-us-about-us.aspx/ (accessed May 3, 2012).

49. Timothy Keller, *Counterfeit Gods: The Empty Promises of Money, Sex, and Power, and the Only Hope That Matters* (New York: Dutton, 2009); David Powlison, "Idols of the Heart and 'Vanity Fair,'" *The Journal of Biblical Counseling* 13, no. 2 (1995): 35–50.

50. David Foster Wallace, "Plain Old Untrendy Troubles and Emotions," *The Guardian*, http://www.guardian.co.uk/books/2008/sep/20/fiction/ (accessed May 3, 2012).

51. Al Barth, "A Vision for Our Cities," Q: Ideas for the Common Good, http://www.qideas.org/blog/a-vision-for-our-cities.aspx/ (accessed May 5, 2012).

52. G. K. Beale, *We Become What We Worship: A Biblical Theology of Idolatry* (Downers Grove, IL: InterVarsity, 2008), 11.

53. Al Barth, "A Vision for Our Cities."

54. Craig L. Blomberg, *Jesus and the Gospels: An Introduction and Survey* (Nashville, TN: Broadman & Holman, 1997), 23.

Chapter 2: The Characteristics of Cities

1. Edward Glaeser, *Triumph of the City: How Our Greatest Invention Makes Us Richer, Smarter, Greener, Healthier, and Happier* (New York: Penguin, 2011), 268.

2. Collin Hansen, "The Stay-Home Generation," The Gospel Coalition, http://thegospelcoalition.org/blogs/tgc/2012/03/18/the-stay-home-generation/ (accessed May 19, 2012).

3. Richard Florida, Who's Your City? How the Creative Economy Is Making Where You Live the Most Important Decision of Your Life (New York: Basic, 2009), 9.

4. William James as quoted by Alain de Botton, Status Anxiety (New York: Vintage International, 2004), 8.

5. Harvie M. Conn and Manuel Ortiz, Urban Ministry: The Kingdom, the City & the People of God (Downers Grove, IL: IVP Academic, 2001), 323–25.

6. Glaeser, Triumph of the City, 70–71.

7. For practical help in this direction, consider Amy L. Sherman, Restorers of Hope: Reaching the Poor in Your Community with Church-based Ministries That Work (Wheaton, IL: Crossway, 1997).

8. Richard Florida's various writings on the "Gay Index" demonstrate that this is the case. Note that on this point we are not seeking to make a moral pronouncement about homosexuality, but are simply pointing to the reality that those who are uncomfortable in a more traditional small-town setting often find themselves pulled toward the city. For helpful discussions on understanding homosexuality from a biblical perspective, refer to Edward T. Welch, Homosexuality: Speaking the Truth in Love, Resources for Changing Lives (Phillipsburg, NJ: P&R, 2000); Andreas J. Kostenberger, God, Marriage, and Family: Rebuilding the Biblical Foundation, 2nd ed. (Wheaton, IL: Crossway, 2010).

9. Conn and Ortiz, Urban Ministry, 88–91.

10. See D. A. Carson, The Intolerance of Tolerance (Grand Rapids, MI: Eerdmans, 2012).

11. Michael Wolfe in New York Magazine, as quoted by Timothy Keller, "Post-everythings," Westminster Theological Seminary, http://www.wts.edu/resources/articles/keller_posteverythings.html/ (accessed May 15, 2012).

12. Richard Florida, The Rise of the Creative Class: And How It's Transforming Work, Leisure, Community and Everyday Life (New York: Basic, 2002), 9.

13. Mark T. Mulder and James K. A. Smith, "Subdivided by Faith? An Historical Account of Evangelicals and the City," Christian Scholars Review 38, no. 4 (2009): 415–33. Mulder and Smith suggest that the largely negative views of the city are rooted in a post–World War II militarism (420).

14. Glaeser claims that our ability to connect with one another is the defining characteristic of our species. Triumph of the City, 269.

15. Ibid., 37.

16. Florida, Who's Your City?, 61ff.

17. For a deeper look at the benefits of density and concentration, not just

for human ingenuity but also for social structures, see chapter 11 of Jane Jacobs, *The Death and Life of Great American Cities* (New York: Modern Library, 1993), 261–89.

18. "Diversity" is being used here in its broadest sense and is not meant to be understood exclusively in terms of ethnic or racial diversity, though it certainly includes those subsets of diversity.

19. The decline of Detroit is well-documented, and the city is often held up as the prime example of American, postindustrial urban decline. See Glaeser, *Triumph of the City*, 52–58; Joel Kotkin, *The City: A Global History* (New York: Modern Library, 2006), 121; Catherine Tumber, *Small, Gritty, and Green: The Promise of America's Smaller Industrial Cities in a Low-Carbon World* (Cambridge, MA: The MIT Press, 2012), xxiii–xxiv. It should be noted here that we are not making a moral judgment on Detroit, the people of Detroit, or the groups and individuals that are working tirelessly to revitalize the city. Our purpose in this section is to illustrate and explain the unfortunate reality that cities do decline, with the hope that an understanding of the root causes of decline will help us better serve our cities. In the ensuing description, we follow the broad contours of Glaeser's thoughts on why cities decline (*Triumph of the City*, 41ff.). An interesting book released during the editing process for *Why Cities Matter* suggests that the one-time collapse of Detroit has made it the ideal laboratory for urban redevelopment. See Mark Binelli, *Detroit Is the Place to Be: The Afterlife of an American Metropolis* (New York: Ballantine, 2012).

20. Jacobs, *The Death and Life of Great American Cities*, 585.

21. Keller develops the like/unlike argument in *Center Church: Doing Balanced, Gospel-Centered Ministry in Your City* (Grand Rapids, MI: Zondervan, 2012), 167–68.

22. Richard Florida has been a champion of the increasingly central role of creativity and ideas. See *The Rise of the Creative Class, Who's Your City?,* and *The Flight of the Creative Class: The New Global Competition for Talent* (New York: HarperCollins, 2005). He suggests that nothing short of a new creative social class has emerged in the last century.

23. L. De Propris, C. Chapain, P. Cooke, S. MacNeill, and J. Mateos-Garcia, "The Geography of Creativity, Interim Report: August 2009," National Endowment for Science, Technology and the Arts, http://www.nesta.org.uk/library/documents/Report%2027%20-%20Geography%20of%20Creativity%20v4.pdf/, 44 (accessed April 26, 2012).

24. Florida, *Who's Your City?,* 27.

25. Ibid.

26. Ibid., 66. The idea of cluster competition has been developed excellently

by Michael E. Porter, *Clusters and the New Economics of Competition* (Boston, MA: Harvard Business Review, 1998).

27. Glaeser, *Triumph of the City*, 6.

28. David Owen, *Green Metropolis: Why Living Smaller, Living Closer, and Driving Less Are the Keys to Sustainability* (New York: Riverhead, 2009). Also, Tumber's *Small, Gritty, and Green.*

29. Glaeser, *Triumph of the City*, 2.

30. Florida, *Who's Your City?*, 13.

31. Jacobs, *The Life and Death of Great American Cities* and Lewis Mumford, *The City in History: Its Origins, Its Transformations, and Its Prospects* (New York: Harcourt, 1961) (although Mumford himself occasionally drifted toward an overly optimistic humanism).

32. Glaeser, *Triumph of the City*, 1.

33. "When it goes well with the righteous, the city rejoices" (Prov. 11:10a). For a wonderfully practical treatment of "rejoicing the city" by seeking the common good in and through one's vocation, see Amy L. Sherman, *Kingdom Calling: Vocational Stewardship for the Common Good* (Downers Grove, IL: InterVarsity, 2011).

34. Glaeser, *Triumph of the City*, 268.

35. Philip Bess in an interview with Paige Smith, "Architecture and Man: A Reciprocal Relationship." Traces: Litterae Communionis, http://www.traces-cl.com/2010/03/architecture.html/ (accessed April 27, 2012). See also Philip Bess, *Till We Have Built Jerusalem: Architecture, Urbanism, and the Sacred* (Wilmington, DE: ISI Books, 2006).

36. As an example of the recent flood of material attempting to address the topic of urbanization, we must cite three books with which we will not have the opportunity to interact. All three were published during the editing process for *Why Cities Matter*. Future research on urbanization will need to take these publications into account: Alan Ehrenhalt, *The Great Inversion and the Future of the American City* (New York: Knopf, 2012); P. D. Smith, *City: A User's Guide to the Past, Present, and Future of Urban Life* (New York: Bloomsbury, 2012); Jeff Speck, *Walkable City: How Downtown Can Save America, One Step at a Time* (New York: Farrar, Straus, and Giroux, 2012).

Chapter 3: The Bible and the City

1. Tim Keller, "A Biblical Theology of the City," The Resurgence, http://theresurgence.com/files/pdf/tim_keller_2002_a_biblical_theology_of_the_city.pdf/ (accessed May 26, 2012).

2. Craig G. Bartholomew, *Where Mortals Dwell: A Christian View of Place Today* (Grand Rapids, MI: Baker Academic, 2011), 2.

3. Edward S. Casey, *Getting Back into Place: Toward a Renewed Understand-*

ing of the Place-World, Studies in Continental Thought (Bloomington, IN: Indiana University Press, 2009), 13.

4. Norbert Lohfink, *Theology of the Pentateuch* (Minneapolis: Fortress, 1994), 10. Cited in Bartholomew, *Where Mortals Dwell*, 13.

5. Gordon J. Spykman, *Reformational Theology: A New Paradigm for Doing Dogmatics* (Grand Rapids, MI: Eerdmans, 1992), 250.

6. Bartholomew, *Where Mortals Dwell*, 3. Cf. Casey, *Getting Back into Place*, 29.

7. Walter Brueggemann, *The Land: Place as Gift, Promise, and Challenge in Biblical Faith* (Philadelphia: Fortress, 1977), 3–4; Edward S. Casey, *The Fate of Place: A Philosophical History* (Berkeley, CA: University of California Press, 1999), ix.

8. Gordon J. Wenham, *Genesis 1–15*, Word Biblical Commentary, vol. 1 (Waco, TX: Word Books, 1987), 1–15, 51–53, 61. The idea of "undeveloped parks" is from Bartholomew, *Where Mortals Dwell*, 26.

9. Bartholomew, *Where Mortals Dwell*, 27.

10. Harvie M. Conn and Manuel Ortiz, *Urban Ministry: The Kingdom, the City & the People of God* (Downers Grove, IL: IVP Academic, 2001), 87.

11. Meredith G. Kline, *Kingdom Prologue*, vol. 2 (South Hamilton, MA: M. G. Kline, 1983), 23.

12. Meredith G. Kline, *Kingdom Prologue: Genesis Foundations for a Covenantal Worldview* (Eugene, OR: Wipf & Stock, 2006), 70.

13. "Indeed, the placial ordering of creation is already indicated in [Genesis] 1:1, in which the heavens and the earth are the objects of God's creative activity." Bartholomew, *Where Mortals Dwell*, 11.

14. Andy Crouch, *Culture Making: Recovering Our Creative Calling* (Downers Grove, IL: InterVarsity, 2008), 104.

15. Leland Ryken, James C. Wilhoit, and Tremper Longman III, eds., "City," *Dictionary of Biblical Imagery* (Downers Grove, IL: InterVarsity, 1998), 150.

16. Meredith Kline, *Kingdom Prologue*, 101, as quoted by Timothy J. Keller, *Center Church: Doing Balanced, Gospel-Centered Ministry in Your City* (Grand Rapids, MI: Zondervan, 2012), 150.

17. "City," *Dictionary of Biblical Imagery*, 153.

18. God's plan for the geographic expansion and cultural development of humanity is clearly seen in Genesis 2:10–14. There we find four rivers that align themselves with the four points of a compass, demonstrating that there are resources beyond the garden that await cultivation. In other words, humanity will have to expand beyond the garden in order to enjoy these natural resources. Furthermore, Genesis provides commentary so that the reader knows where to find the best resources. So, follow the Pishon River and you will find gold, bdellium, and onyx stone (vv. 11–12). It is no mistake that we find these and other resources in the fully cul-

tivated, eschatological garden city of Revelation 21. Andy Crouch puts it this way: "Readers with a keen and long memory will note that the natural resources nearby the original Garden in Genesis 2 are . . . in the new Jerusalem as well [Rev. 21:18–21] . . . The gold has been put to use; the onyx is one of the many jewels that make up a city's foundations; and the bdellium, a tree gum . . . that hardened into translucent white balls that were prized as jewelry . . . , is echoed in the twelve pearls that form the gates to the city. The natural riches that surrounded the Garden have been cultivated and brought to their most striking expression for the city's adornment." *Culture Making*, 165.

19. Tim Keller, unpublished notes.
20. Conn and Ortiz, *Urban Ministry*, 237.
21. Don C. Benjamin, *Deuteronomy and City Life: A Form Criticism of Texts with the Word CITY ('îr) in Deuteronomy 4:41–26:19* (Lanham, MD: University Press of America, 1983), 23. Though Benjamin's form critical approach yields mixed results, the core of his thesis shows that nomadism was never the ideal for Israel. "*Deuteronomy and City Life* describes Israel as an *urban culture*. . . . Israel was at times migrant, and itinerant, and pastoral, but she was not nomadic, because she was always going somewhere. The history and the life and the hope of Israel as a culture centers on Yahweh's promise to lead her into a land where she may be secure, and the core of this land with which the destiny of ancient Israel is so closely tied is the city!" (23).
22. For some development of the idea that Christians ought to have a "faithful presence" in the world, see James Davidson Hunter, *To Change the World: The Irony, Tragedy, and Possibility of Christianity in a Late Modern World* (New York: Oxford University Press, 2010).
23. Conn and Ortiz, *Urban Ministry*, 121, citing J. Andrew Overman, "Who Were the First Urban Christians? Urbanization in Galilee in the First Century," SBL Seminar Papers, ed. David Lull (Atlanta: Scholars Press, 1988), 165.
24. For a helpful discussion of the implications of Jesus being identified as the new temple, see G. K. Beale, *The Temple and the Church's Mission: A Biblical Theology of the Dwelling Place of God*, New Studies in Biblical Theology (Downers Grove, IL: InterVarsity, 2004), 169–200.
25. Conn and Ortiz, *Urban Ministry*, 122.
26. Jesus understood his own death to be the destruction of the temple (John 2:19).
27. An adaptation of a thought from Keller, *Center Church*, 179.
28. Of the 160 times the Greek word *polis*, or city, is used in the New Testament, 80 of those occurrences (50 percent) are found in the Lukan writ-

ings. Luke is so concerned to highlight cities that he goes out of his way to use *polis* where other writers are content to use less descriptive words. For more, see Conn and Ortiz, *Urban Ministry*, 123–25.

29. Rodney Stark, *Cities of God: The Real Story of How Christianity Became an Urban Movement and Conquered Rome* (New York: HarperCollins, 2006), suggests that it did.
30. See Beale, *The Temple and the Church's Mission*, 81–87.
31. "City," *Dictionary of Biblical Imagery*, 153 (emphasis added).
32. John R. W. Stott, *The Message of Acts*, The Bible Speaks Today (Downers Grove, IL: IVP Academic, 1994), 293.
33. Conn and Ortiz, *Urban Ministry*, 128.
34. As cited in ibid., 129.
35. Rodney Stark, *The Rise of Christianity: How the Obscure, Marginal Jesus Movement Became the Dominant Religious Force in the Western World in a Few Centuries* (San Francisco: HarperSanFrancisco, 1997). Believers stayed in the city when there were plagues, etc.
36. For those still unconvinced, consider Paul's use of the phrase "kingdom" or "kingdom of God." Based on the fact that Paul does not often use kingdom terminology (only 14 times in all of his letters, compared to 134 occurrences elsewhere in the New Testament), some have sought to propose a divide between Jesus's gospel of the kingdom and Paul's gospel of salvation. Jesus continually spoke of a present and coming kingdom. Paul only rarely speaks of the kingdom, and when he does he is likely to see it as something in the future that we ought to avoid being disqualified from by way immorality (Gal. 5:21; Eph. 5:5). Is there a disconnect here? Did Jesus and Paul have different understandings of the gospel and the kingdom? No. Rather, much like he assumes his readers are in the context of the city, so Paul assumes that the members of the churches he is writing to are already in the kingdom of God (Col. 1:13). The kingdom is the context within which they are all living. The absence of explicit statements about context does not define context. The way that Paul talks about the kingdom is via lordship language.
37. Wayne A. Meeks, *The First Urban Christians: The Social World of the Apostle Paul*, 2nd ed. (New Haven, CT: Yale University Press, 2003), 9.
38. "You have come" is in the perfect tense. In other words, the Christian's coming to the city of the living God is "an event that, completed in the past . . . , has results existing in the present time." Daniel B. Wallace, *Greek Grammar Beyond the Basics: An Exegetical Syntax of the New Testament* (Grand Rapids, MI: Zondervan, 1996), 573.
39. G. K. Beale, *A New Testament Biblical Theology: The Unfolding of the Old Testament in the New* (Grand Rapids, MI: Baker Academic, 2011), 143.

40. Keller, *Center Church*, 146. "Resident aliens" is a term borrowed from Stanley Hauerwas and William H. Willimon, *Resident Aliens: Life in the Christian Colony* (Nashville, TN: Abingdon, 1989).
41. "Compared with [the future Jerusalem], all earthly cities are mere temporary tent camps. . . . The earthly Jerusalem is only a copy and a shadow or a symbol of the city which is to come." Hans Bietenhard, "People," *The New International Dictionary of New Testament Theology*, vol. 2, ed. Colin Brown (Grand Rapids, MI: Zondervan, 1979), 803.
42. Keller, *Center Church*, 179.

Chapter 4: Contextualization in the City

1. D. A. Carson, "Maintaining Scientific and Christian Truths in a Postmodern World," *Science & Christian Belief* 14, no. 2 (2002): 107–22.
2. Post-Christian societies are cultures where the Christian worldview was once the dominant worldview. Many European cities were once known for having a thriving Christian influence and a population that largely subscribed to the central tenets of Christian orthodoxy. Take London, for example. One hundred years ago the majority of Londoners were coming at life from the same page, with the same general convictions about life, God, and orthodoxy. Today's London looks very different from the London of one hundred years ago, as only a small percentage of the city's population identifies as being Christian. London is a post-Christian city. Many would also classify major American cities such as New York City, San Francisco, and the Silicon Valley region as post-Christian because these cities have also experienced decline. For example, the church that my (Justin's) church plant rents space from for our Sunday services was once a thriving church. It was planted in 1898 with a vision to reach San Jose with the gospel. In 1926 that church bought property (the current facility we use) in the heart of San Jose. In 1926 the population of San Jose was 48,000 people. This church grew along with the city—many were converted through the ministry of the church, attendance soared, and the church planted several churches throughout the growing Silicon Valley. But today the population of San Jose is over one million, making San Jose the tenth largest city in America, and this church is a shadow of its former self, home to about sixty worshipers on an average Sunday. So, yes, American cities are full of stories like this of diminishing Christian influence and could be classified as post-Christian. But we hesitate to use the label "post-Christian" for American cities. While we see a general post-Christian trajectory, American cities have not yet experienced the same degree of decline as European cities.
3. The classic work on this topic is Augustine's *City of God*. Written in the fifth century AD to instruct Christians on how to live within a collapsing

Roman Empire, and eventually becoming a voluminous philosophy of history, this remains an important book for Christians.

4. Cornelius Plantinga, *Not the Way It's Supposed to Be: A Breviary of Sin* (Grand Rapids, MI: Eerdmans, 1995), 10; cf. Nicholas Wolterstorff, *Until Justice and Peace Embrace: The Kuyper Lectures for 1981 Delivered at the Free University of Amsterdam* (Grand Rapids, MI: Eerdmans, 1983), 69–72.

5. We are not denigrating the existence of institutions such as Christian bookstores or Christian schools, but simply pointing out that many such institutions tend to isolate themselves from culture rather than engage it.

6. Ray Bakke, *A Theology as Big as the City* (Downers Grove, IL: InterVarsity Press, 1997), 14.

7. We don't mean to communicate that culture is not also shaped in regions that are not classified as cities. Our point is that the most significant culture shaping happens in cities because more people live in cities.

8. Keller, *Center Church: Doing Balanced, Gospel-Centered Ministry in Your City* (Grand Rapids, MI: Zondervan, 2012), 88.

9. Bill Crispin, as quoted by "Food for Urban Thought," A City Lit by Fireflies (blog), January 16, 2008, http://citylitbyfireflies.blogspot.com/2008/01 /food-for-urban-thought.html/ (accessed April 30, 2012).

10. For the distinction between institutional and organic church, see "The Spheres and Roles of the Church" in Keller, *Center Church*, 294–95.

11. D. A. Carson on the difference between the gospel and its entailments: "The gospel is the good news of what God has done, especially in Christ Jesus, especially in his cross and resurrection; it is not what we do. Because it is news, it is to be proclaimed. But because it is powerful, it not only reconciles us to God, but transforms us, and that *necessarily* shapes our behavior, priorities, values, relationships with people, and much more. These are not optional extras for the extremely sanctified, but *entailments* of the gospel." Don Carson, "TGC Asks Don Carson: How Do We Work for Justice and Not Undermine Evangelism?" The Gospel Coalition, http://thegospelcoalition.org/blogs/tgc/2010/10/18/asks-carson-jus tice-evangelism/ (accessed May 25, 2012).

12. Tim Keller, "Preaching the Gospel," *PT 123: Gospel Communication* (course for Westminster Theological Seminary, Spring 2003), 33–34.

13. Contextualization is one of the most important topics of discussion in evangelical circles today. For a good overview of the issues at play, consider by Keller, *Center Church*, 89–134. We would follow Keller in saying that "sound contextualization means translating and adapting the communication and ministry of the gospel to a particular culture without compromising the essence and particulars of the gospel itself" (89).

14. Keller, *Center Church*, 24.
15. Richard Florida, *Who's Your City? How the Creative Economy Is Making Where You Live the Most Important Decision of Your Life* (New York: Basic, 2009).
16. For a recent attempt to expand the traditional borders of Silicon Valley, see Chris O'Brien, "What We Call Silicon Valley Now Includes S. F., East Bay," *San Jose Mercury News*, April 22, 2012.
17. For more on the history of San Jose, see Edwin A. Beilharz and Donald O. DeMers Jr., *San Jose: California's First City* (Tulsa, OK: Continental Heritage Press, 1980).
18. I (Justin) named my church "Garden City Church" in order to resurrect the old name of our city, and because the Bible is a book that starts in a garden and ends in a Garden City. Go to www.GardenCitySV.com for more information.
19. There is not space in this book to address the Native American history that predates the settlement of San Jose.
20. Felipe de Neve reporting in a letter to Viceroy Antonio Maria de Bucareli on the founding of San Jose. Beilharz and DeMers, *San Jose*, 23.
21. For more, see Tim Stanley, *The Last of the Prune Pickers: A Pre-Silicon Valley Story* (Irvine, CA: 2 Timothy Publishing, 2010).
22. Thomas Chatterton Williams, "Bookshelf: Dark Thoughts in City of Light," *The Wall Street Journal*, May 1, 2012.
23. Peter Newcomb, "Reid Hoffman," *The Wall Street Journal Magazine*, June 23, 2011.
24. Edward Glaeser, *Triumph of the City: How Our Greatest Invention Makes Us Richer, Smarter, Greener, Healthier, and Happier* (New York: Penguin, 2011), 188–89.
25. Saskia Sassen makes this observation throughout *The Global City: New York, London, Tokyo* (Princeton, NJ: Princeton University Press, 2001).
26. Most of Silicon Valley is built around the car, yet there are many exceptions. I (Justin) currently live in a walkable, mixed-use region of Silicon Valley. Within a quarter-mile radius of my front door I can walk to scores of businesses, coffee shops, restaurants, a school, a park, the post office, a fire station, places of worship, a cemetery, and hiking trails, and cross paths with a great diversity of people. The section of the city where our church holds Sunday services functions the same—walkable, mixed-use, and highly diverse. This is a good place to recall what the biblical writers meant by "city." "What makes a city a city is proximity. It brings people—and therefore residences, workplaces, and cultural institutions—together. It creates street life and marketplaces, bringing about more person-to-person interactions and exchanges in a day than

are possible anywhere else. This is what the Biblical writers meant when they talked about a 'city.'" Tim Keller, "What Is God's Global Urban Mission?" *The Lausanne Movement* (advance paper, Lausanne 2010, Cape Town, South Africa, May 18, 2010), http://conversation.lausanne.org/en/conversations/detail/10282#article_page_5.

27. Glaeser, *Triumph of the City*, 32–33.
28. Jonathan Lehrer and Richard Florida, "How Creativity Works in Cities," The Atlantic Cities, http://www.theatlanticcities.com/arts-and-lifestyle/2012/05/how-creativity-works/1881/ (accessed May 8, 2012).
29. Glaeser, *Triumph of the City*, 34.
30. Keller, *Center Church*, 90–91.
31. Jonathan Dodson, "Five Things New Planters Should Know," Acts 29 Network, http://www.acts29network.org/acts-29-blog/five-things-new-planters-should-know/ (accessed May 18, 2012).

Chapter 5: The Story Line of the City

1. Leonardo de Chirico, "Identifying the Idols of the City," Q: Ideas for the Common Good, http://www.qideas.org/blog/identifying-the-idols-of-the-city.aspx/ (accessed May 3, 2012).
2. Estimates are that Jerusalem had a population of about thirty thousand during the ministry of Jesus. A population of thirty thousand was a large-sized city for the first-century Roman world. In the first-century Roman Empire, only two major cities had populations of more than 150,000: Rome and Alexandria. Rome had a population of 450,000 and a density of 200 to 300 people per acre. Rodney Stark, *Cities of God: The Real Story of How Christianity Became an Urban Movement and Conquered Rome* (New York: HarperCollins, 2006), 26–27, 52.
3. Keller identifies six different types of audiences that Paul contextualizes the gospel to in the book of Acts: Bible believers, peasant polytheists, sophisticated pagans, Christian elders, a hostile Jewish mob, and governing elites Timothy J. Keller, *Center Church: Doing Balanced, Gospel-Centered Ministry in Your City* (Grand Rapids, MI: Zondervan, 2012), 112.
4. Ultimately, the kingdom of God advances in our cities only as a result of a sovereign work of God. Nevertheless, God uses means, and the New Testament documents bear witness to how God used the apostle Paul's retelling of a city's story line (sensitive and thoughtful contextualized preaching of the gospel) to significantly advance the kingdom. This means/method also shows up throughout church history. For instance, note how often this theme shows up in some of history's greatest revival stories in Collin Hansen and John Woodbridge, *A God-Sized Vision: Revival Stories That Stretch and Stir* (Grand Rapids, MI: Zondervan, 2010).

5. Tim Keller argues for a similar three-part process to active contextualization: entering the culture, challenging the culture, and appealing to the listeners. *Center Church*, 120.

6. Edward Glaeser, *Triumph of the City: How Our Greatest Invention Makes Us Richer, Smarter, Greener, Healthier, and Happier* (New York: Penguin, 2011), 15.

7. Timothy Keller, "Our New Global Culture: Ministry in Urban Centers" (New York: Redeemer City to City, 2010), 2.

8. The following is a good example of how the success story line dominates the atmosphere of Silicon Valley: "Silicon Valley has become the twenty-first-century model for entrepreneurship and progress and has had multiple generations of entrepreneurial companies over the decades: from Hewlett Packard's founding in 1939 to Intel, Apple, Adobe, Genentech, AMD, Intuit, Oracle, Electronic Arts, Pixar, and Cisco, and then to Google, eBay, Yahoo, Seagate, and Salesforce, and then more recently to PayPal, Facebook, YouTube, Craigslist, Twitter, and LinkedIn. . . . In each passing decade, Silicon Valley has kept and intensified its entrepreneurial mojo, with dozens of companies creating the future and adapting to the evolution of the global market. These companies provide not only a new model for corporate innovation, but also the entrepreneur mind-set needed to succeed in individual careers." Reid Hoffman and Ben Casnocha, *The Start-Up of You* (New York: Crown, 2012), 18.

9. Margery Turner, vice president for research at The Urban Institute, recently graded America's one hundred biggest metropolitan areas on "how much economic security they offer families in these tough times." Oklahoma City came out on top. Russ Pillman, Brandon Dutcher, and Edward Lee Pitts, "Joining the Big Leagues," *World*, March 10, 2012, 60.

10. Surprisingly, India is not heavily urbanized. "In India, only 31.3 percent of its 1.24 billion people live in urban areas. That is below the level of neighboring Pakistan (36.2 percent). It is also well below the level for the Southern Asia region as a whole (32.6 percent), which in addition to India and Pakistan includes highly urbanized Iran, where 69.1 percent of the population is urban." "Globalist Quiz: Urban Population Dynamics," *San Jose Mercury News*, April 22, 2012.

11. This observation comes from Makoto Fukuda and Geert de Boo of Grace City Church Tokyo (http://www.gracecitychurch.jp/english/). Geert observes, "'Collective' does capture the dominant cultural storyline, but . . . 'conformity' is even closer. It reflects a deeper motivation or drive of why the collective is made so important. Conforming to the group makes one belong, providing identity and meaning. That is why Japanese society is characterized by such a monolithic culture. The nuance is that col-

lective is only important when it is the *kachi-gumi* (the winners). Those who cannot conform (enough) are the *make-gumi* (losers) and this dynamic (of trying *not* to be different) is what deeply drives this society. The importance of the collective over the individual radiates a beauty lost mostly in the West. Yet the drive is an equally self-centered one and in need of the same gospel of grace."

12. Many Westerners have not heard of Lagos. Situated on the coast of Nigeria, Lagos is the largest city in Africa, home to more than twelve million people. Lagos is growing fast. By 2050, economists predict Nigeria will be the world's fourth most populous nation. Mindy Belz, "Stressed-Out Cities," *World,* March 10, 2012, 49.

13. During Detroit's golden age, it was the fourth most populous city in America and the city's median income was the highest in America. "Detroit boasted a diversity, energy, culture, and progressive spirit that rivaled Chicago and New York. . . . It was the first city to assign individual telephone numbers, pave a mile of concrete road, and develop an urban freeway. In the 1940s, '50s, and '60s, Detroit was a crown jewel of America." Hoffman and Casnocha, *The Start-Up of You,* 13–14. Today's Detroit is a far cry from its former self, but the city is being slowly rebuilt under a story line of hope.

14. Michael Wines, "Johannesburg Rises Above Its Apartheid Past," *The New York Times,* http://travel.nytimes.com/2006/07/16/travel/16next.htmlpagewanted=all/ (accessed April 10, 2012).

15. "Introduction to 1 Thessalonians," *ESV Study Bible* (Wheaton, IL: Crossway, 2007), 2301. Again, one hundred thousand was a very large metropolitan population in the first century.

16. Richard Lints suggests that the idolatrous stories of our time are inevitably synthetic or "vinyl" narratives: "The vinyl narratives of our times suggest that reality is eminently moldable into our own image, that our image is profoundly flexible and ought to be shaped according to our deepest desires, and finally that those desires are most fruitful when empowered with choice." It is the church's task to hold out the story of God's work in redemptive history as the true alternative to all imitators. "The redemptive narrative of Scripture is . . . a story which . . . continues to interpret all of life through its structures." Richard Lints, "The Vinyl Narratives: The Metanarrative of Postmodernity and the Recovery of a Churchly Theology" in *A Confessing Theology for Postmodern Times,* ed. Michael S. Horton (Wheaton, IL: Crossway, 2000), 95, 99.

17. One of the best short treatments on idolatry is chapter 12 ("Idol-Shattering") of Darrin Patrick, *Church Planter: The Man, The Message, The Mission* (Wheaton, IL: Crossway, 2010). For a more thorough treatment

see Timothy Keller, *Counterfeit Gods: The Empty Promises of Money, Sex, and Power, and the Only Hope That Matters* (New York: Dutton, 2009) and G. K. Beale, *We Become What We Worship: A Biblical Theology of Idolatry* (Downers Grove, IL: InterVarsity, 2008).

18. Leonardo de Chirico, "Identifying the Idols of the City." He goes on to state: "Observation is key to discerning the presence of idols in the city. Full immersion is indispensable. This requires reading the history of the city from different points of view. Becoming familiar with its maps, cultural history, geography, spirituality, politics, art, food, social dynamics, trends, demography, literature, institutionalized religion, movements, and so on, is part and parcel of the task. To identify city idols we should be culturally omnivorous, since idolatry is present everywhere in culture."

19. Andy Sambidge, "Dubai Ranks Top for Luxury Homes in Wealth Index," Arabian Business.com, http://www.arabianbusiness.com/dubai-ranks -top-for-luxury-homes-in-wealth-index-18363.html/ (accessed April 25, 2012).

20. Wikipedia, "List of Tourist Attractions in Dubai," http://en.wikipedia. org/wiki/List_of_tourist_attractions_in_Dubai (accessed April 25, 2012).

21. Gloria Furman, e-mail message to Justin Buzzard, May 4, 2012.

22. Keller, *Center Church*, 121.

23. As quoted in Glaeser, *Triumph of the City*, 118.

24. David Cody, "A Brief History of London," *Victorian Web*, http://www.vic torianweb.org/history/hist4.html/ (accessed May 6, 2012).

25. William Kilpatrick, *Why Johnny Can't Tell Right from Wrong* (New York: Simon & Schuster, 1993).

Chapter 6: Ministry Vision for the City

1. These questions and statistics are recounted in Alan Hirsch, *The Forgotten Ways: Reactivating the Missional Church* (Grand Rapids, MI: Baker, 2006), 18. Hirsch's research relies heavily on Stark's *The Rise of Christianity: How the Obscure, Marginal Jesus Movement Became the Dominant Religious Force in the Western World in a Few Centuries* (San Francisco: HarperSanFrancisco, 1997).

2. Rodney Stark, *Cities of God: The Real Story of How Christianity Became an Urban Movement and Conquered Rome* (New York: HarperCollins, 2006), 2.

3. Ibid., 25–26.

4. Al Barth, "A Vision for Our Cities," Q: Ideas for the Common Good, http:// www.qideas.org/blog/a-vision-for-our-cities.aspx/ (accessed May 5, 2012).

5. McKinsey Global Institute, *Urban World: Mapping the Economic Power of Cities*, March 2011.

6. Edward Glaeser, *Triumph of the City: How Our Greatest Invention Makes*

Us Richer, Smarter, Greener, Healthier, and Happier (New York: Penguin, 2011), 1.

7. Matt Carter and Darrin Patrick, *For the City: Proclaiming and Living Out the Gospel* (Grand Rapids, MI: Zondervan, 2010), 24.

8. Taken from The Gospel Coalition's confessional statement in D. A. Carson and Timothy Keller, eds., *The Gospel as Center: Renewing Our Faith and Reforming Our Ministry Practices* (Wheaton, IL: Crossway, 2012), 276. Carson's article, "The Gospel of Jesus Christ (1 Corinthians 15:1–19)," is an extended treatment of this statement, and is available at *The Spurgeon Fellowship Journal*, http://www.thespurgeonfellowship.org/Spring08 /journal_home.htm. An even more concise way to sum up the gospel is suggested by Tim Keller, drawing on Simon Gathercole's three-point outline: "Through the person and work of Jesus Christ, God fully accomplishes salvation for us, rescuing us from judgment for sin into fellowship with him, and then restores the creation in which we can enjoy our new life together with him forever." Timothy Keller, "The Gospel in All Its Forms," *Leadership Journal* (Spring 2008), http://www.christianity today.com/le/2008/spring/9.74a.html/.

9. This section is indebted to Keller's "The Gospel in All Its Forms."

10. Timothy J. Keller, *Center Church: Doing Balanced, Gospel-Centered Ministry in Your City* (Grand Rapids, MI: Zondervan, 2012), 28.

11. For more on the personal nature of the gospel, see chapter 7 of Justin Buzzard, *Date Your Wife* (Wheaton, IL: Crossway, 2012).

12. Along these lines, we have found many churches in our cities that proclaim a false gospel that amounts to "a God without wrath brings men without sin into a kingdom without judgment through Christ without a cross." H. Richard Niebuhr, *The Kindgom of God in America* (Middletown, CT: Wesleyan, 1988), 193.

13. Randy Frazee, *The Connecting Church: Beyond Small Groups to Authentic Community* (Grand Rapids, MI: Zondervan, 2001), 46–47.

14. Taken from Garden City Church, core values, http://www.gardencity sanjose.com/#/about/values/.

15. Glaeser, *Triumph of the City*, 269.

16. Tim Keller, *Gospel in Life: Grace Changes Everything* (Grand Rapids, MI: Zondervan, 2010), 69.

17. An in-depth discussion on the nature of discipleship is beyond the scope of this book. For helpful resources see Jonathan Dodson, *Gospel-Centered Discipleship* (Wheaton, IL: Crossway, 2012), as well as Gary Parrett and S. Steve Kang, *Teaching the Faith, Forming the Faithful: A Biblical Vision for Education in the Church* (Downers Grove, IL: InterVarsity, 2009).

18. Rodney Stark, *The Rise of Christianity*, 161–62.

19. There is not space in this book to deal with all of the complex issues at play when we consider the church's relationship to ministries of mercy and justice. We are advocating for a posture that errs on the side of generosity in response to the gospel, while also respecting the natural limitations of the institutional church. For more, see Timothy Keller, *Generous Justice: How God's Grace Makes Us Just* (New York: Dutton, 2010); Steve Corbett and Brian Fikkert, *When Helping Hurts: How to Alleviate Poverty without Hurting the Poor . . . and Yourself* (Chicago: Moody, 2012).

20. Tim Keller, "What Is God's Global Urban Mission?," *The Lausanne Movement* (advance paper, Lausanne 2010, Cape Town, South Africa, May 18, 2010), http://conversation.lausanne.org/en/conversations/detail/10282 #article_page_5.

21. Ray Bakke, *A Theology as Big as the City* (Downers Grove, IL: InterVarsity Press, 1997), 34.

22. A very helpful resource in this regard is Amy Sherman's *Kingdom Calling* (Downers Grove, IL: InterVarsity, 2011). One church we're in relationship with that is doing a particularly good job of what we're talking about here is The Austin Stone Community Church (http://austinstone.org/) in Austin, Texas. To further their mission to the city, Austin Stone started a nonprofit, For the City Network (http://forthecity.org/), which connects individuals, churches, and communities to city restoration efforts that range from caring for orphans, rebuilding broken neighborhoods, mentoring underprivileged youth, and caring for the homeless.

23. Keller, *Center Church*, 291.

24. C. Peter Wagner, *Strategies for Church Growth: Tools for Effective Mission and Evangelism* (Ventura, CA: Regal, 1987), 168–69.

25. See Redeemer City to City, http://redeemercitytocity.com/.

26. See Acts 29 Network, http://www.acts29network.org/.

27. I (Justin) planted my church in partnership with four networks: the Acts 29 Network; Fellowship Associates (http://www.fellowshipassociates .org/); Vision 360 (http://vision360.org/); and the NorCal Network (http:// norcalnetwork.org/).

28. Keller, "What Is God's Global Urban Mission?"

29. "The Letter to Diognetus," Christian Classics Ethereal Library, http:// www.ccel.org/ccel/richardson/fathers.x.i.ii.html/ (accessed May 15, 2012).

30. Augustine, *City of God: An Abridged Version*, ed. Vernon J. Bourke (New York: Doubleday, 1958), 540–45.

31. For additional resources and information on speaking engagements, visit the authors' respective websites (http://www.justinbuzzard.net/; http://centerforgospelculture.org/).

GENERAL INDEX

SCRIPTURE INDEX